Make Your Job Great

How to Step Up, Own Your Space & Get Your Boss off Your Back

By Joanne Eckton

Nashville, TN 37080

Reach the Author at:

www.MakeYourJobGreat.com

email: Joanne@LifeChoiceExpert.com

Table of Contents

ACKNOWLEDGMENTS

This book would never have materialized without the support from two wonderful people I have the good fortune to call friend:

Omar Periu, Omar Periu International, whose advice, feedback and encouragement helped me to keep my doubts in check.

Roger Salam, CEO of The Winners Circle, who changed my belief system and first helped me realize that I too could write a book of my own.

I also owe a special debt of gratitude to Dawn Clark, who painstakingly edited these pages and provided insights that helped polish this book into the final version you are reading today.

DEDICATION

This book is dedicated to my husband, Paris, who has always believed in me and supported me, and to my best friend, Kathy, who pushed me for years to write this and would not take no for an answer. Thank you both for your constant love and encouragement.

Get Your Life Back!

Subscribe to our Ezine Today! Free newsletter is full of tips and strategies for defining success your way.

You'll also receive:

* Expert Interviews with successful business leaders who share their secrets with you

* A complimentary copy of our amazing e-book, Successful Entrepreneur Secrets: Engage Your Workforce to Create the Business of Your Dreams

To sign up, go to LifeChoiceExpert.com

Introduction

Our workforce today is full of people who are drifting, going through the motions of showing up for work each day, doing what they are told, reacting to whatever demands others make of them during the day, and going home with no real feeling of satisfaction.

It is said that 95% of people go home from work unsatisfied. You don't have to be one of them.

If you are unhappy at work, you have two choices: you can either change your situation or change your reaction to that situation. Unfortunately, most people do neither and live out their days without enthusiasm. Worse, they spend their time complaining, bringing negativity into their lives. With the principles in this book, you can make positive changes that will improve your situation and help you be happier at work.

Consider these scenarios:

.... young employees not equipped to enter the workforce, with no work ethic and a shocking lack of initiative

.... a rising star at work that fizzles out over time

.... employees who complain about the incompetence of their bosses

.... a teenager in her first minimum wage job who recognizes that other teenagers there are slow or just plain lazy

.... a highly paid, qualified professional that only does what the boss tells him to do

.... staff that won't work with specific individuals because they know they won't hold up their end

With the strategies in this book, you will have the tools to rise above these problems and more. Bring out the best in yourself and become a superstar.

All of these are symptoms of a larger problem: expecting someone else to make everything better. The truly successful, those who are enthusiastic about what they do, understand that the only way to get what you want out of life is to step up and make it happen yourself.

When you were at the stage in your life where you were finishing high school, people started asking you questions about what you wanted to do with the rest of your life. What did you want to be? If you were planning to go to college, what major were you going to choose?

Chances are you had no real idea, right? If you are like most people, you just took your best guess.

There are a few who are passionate about something and know exactly what they want. This book is not written for them.

The rest of us tend to take the path of least resistance. Most likely, you picked a field you were familiar with, similar to what one of your parents did, or you took the first job that you could get. In my case, I did both. I always wanted to be "in computers." When I was a kid, my dad would take me into his office on Saturdays and I'd spend the day fascinated with the computers while my dad did whatever it was he was there to do. When it was time for me to get my first full-time *serious* job, though, I took the first one that came along. It had nothing to do with computers. I spent six months in a field that I had no interest in, other than receiving a paycheck. Luckily for me, right at the time that firm went bankrupt I got a call from a job application I'd submitted months earlier. This time the job was in my chosen field, and from that point forward I made (mostly) well thought out and intentional job changes that helped me to advance in my career.

Over the years, I've worked with hundreds of people who let circumstances dictate what they do for a living. These are the people you hear about, that spend more time planning a vacation than they do on planning their careers. They live up to the expectations of others, and do not invest the time to figure out what drives them. Eventually, they wake up and find themselves miserable at work and don't know what to do about it.

This book is not about how to find your dream job. It's about how to transform yourself at work so that you are proud of what you do, excited to go to work on Monday morning, and feel good at the end of the day, every day.

It's time to look at the person you are when you show up at work and revitalize, embolden and empower that person to take charge of your professional life.

Let's get started.

Excellence is never an accident. It is always the result of high intention, sincere effort, and intelligent execution; it represents the wise choice of many alternatives - choice, not chance, determines your destiny."

— Aristotle

Part A: Know Your Space

Chapter 1: You Have to Earn Your Freedom

He only earns his freedom and his life
who takes them every day by storm.

—Johann Wolfgang von Goethe

Your boss stinks? Is he always breathing down your neck, telling you what to do, and then staying on your back until it gets done? Do you wish he would just leave you alone?

Well, guess what? Chances are your boss is frustrated with you also.

You have to earn your freedom. People want autonomy in their jobs, but the harsh reality is you have to earn it. Most bosses do not enjoy micro-managing, but they do this out of fear. Fear that the work isn't getting done properly. Fear that HIS boss will start breathing down his neck looking for results. All your boss wants is someone he can turn his back on and know that whatever it is you are responsible for will get done. And that it will be done correctly, accurately and on time.

If you need to be told what to do and then consistently asked for status until the task is finally done, your boss has no alternative but to micromanage you. On the other hand, if you

Make Your Job Great

are the kind of person who is proactive, who looks at what needs to be done and then tackles it, then your boss will have less need to watch over you. If you want more latitude in your job, be the kind of person your boss can trust to get the work done.

Early in her career, Cary had a supervisor who understood this and rewarded it. She was a computer programmer who showed up for work later than most of the team because she was usually up late the night before. One day, her boss called her into a conference room, and she was sure she was about to get "the talk" about her working hours. Instead, he gave her an award! His comments were that he recognized that every time there was a tough problem that needed to be solved, regardless of whether it was during working hours, late night or on the weekend, Cary was the one he could count on to fix it. He did not care that she strolled into work at 10am, he cared about the results she was getting.

It's been proven, time and time again, that employees who get results, who can be trusted to get the work done, have much more freedom from the bureaucracy imposed by management and more success in their careers.

You will earn your freedom when you have consistently demonstrated that you:

- Take care of your responsibilities to meet or exceed expectations
- Complete work accurately and on time
- Provide regular status updates
- Raise issues when you need help

That's it.

The first step towards earning your freedom is in getting absolutely clear on your boss's expectations. If you don't know what he is holding you responsible for, you'll be shooting in the dark. At this point, if you are ready to run to your boss and ask him what his expectations are, don't! At best you'll get a half-baked answer. Your boss is busy, he has many other things on his mind, and an impromptu discussion of roles and responsibilities will not get the time and attention it deserves.

Here's an example of how that conversation might go:

Tom: *Hey boss, do you have a few minutes? I'd like to talk to you about my responsibilities.*

Rita: *What's the problem? You know you were hired to put together our executive presentations, and you're doing a great job at that. Is someone asking you to do something else?*

Tom: *No, but I wanted to be clear on your expectations of me.*

Rita: *I'm late for a meeting, but you have nothing to worry about. You're doing just fine.*

Tom didn't get any real feedback from his boss, and she barely acknowledged the conversation because her mind was elsewhere. These kinds of conversations happen all the time in companies, and they do not accomplish a thing. The employee wants to talk in detail, but the boss is rushing from one thing to the next and gives him the equivalent of a verbal pat on the head.

The professional will draft up a document first, outlining each responsibility, the timing, and the answer to "how do I know this is done?" Focus on the entire deliverable, not just the tasks that you personally need to do. From your manager's perspective, the work isn't done until everyone's pieces are done. Help make this happen by focusing on the big picture, not just your space.

For example, here is a very simplified version that a software developer might use:

Overall Target: Deliver computer program for Module XYZ

Tasks:

1. Code checked in configuration management tool
2. Design published in library
3. User training materials produced
4. Test scripts written
5. Test scripts 100% passed
6. Training executed
7. Software installed

The software developer might only be responsible for the first task or two, but the software cannot be considered completed until all the steps are done.

It is up to you to draft this list to the best of your ability, and set an appointment with your boss to review it. Ask if he wants a copy of the list to review ahead of time. Some people are analytical types that want time to study the document and get their thoughts together. More realistically, your boss will not even look at the document for more than a few minutes before your meeting, so it is important that you make sure he is able to dedicate some focused time with you and not be distracted by the urgent matters of the day.

During the meeting, ask your boss what else should be added to the list. What else can you do to help the department run better, or to offload responsibility from your boss? This is where you are likely to get the best feedback. To continue the example of the computer programmer above, he could make the work flow better by reviewing the design with the test team to make sure they understand it, and then communicating with them when the code has been checked in so they know they can begin their testing cycles. Rather than focusing just on what the programmer needs to do to finish his part of the work, his boss is more interested in making sure all the steps are completed so that the module can be shipped to the customer. How can you think beyond your immediate deliverables to the larger picture?

Back to Tom and Rita and how the revised conversation might flow:

Tom: *Rita, can we schedule 30 minutes to get together to talk about my responsibilities?*

Rita: *Is there a problem? You know you were hired to put together our executive presentations, and you're doing a great job at that. Is someone asking you to do something else?*

Tom: *No, but I've drafted a list of everything I think you need me to do, and I want to be sure we are in agreement so that I can meet your expectations.*

Rita: *Ok, sure. My Outlook calendar is up to date, so just schedule something on my calendar.*

During the meeting, Tom will need to guide the conversation to get the results he needs. However, by scheduling the meeting ahead of time and letting his boss know what the topic of conversation will be he's come a lot closer to having a true discussion.

Tom: *Rita, thank you for spending some time with me to talk about my responsibilities.*

Rita: *No problem. What exactly is your concern?*

Tom: *I know overall you need me to help with executive presentations, but I wanted to review in detail what I should be doing to help you. I sent you a copy of the list I drafted, but just in case you haven't had time to look at it here's a copy for us to use today.*

Rita: *You're right, I've only just glanced at it, and frankly, I'm not sure what you are looking for.*

Tom: *I know what I was hired to do. What I'd really like to review with you is what your expectations are for completing this work so that I can completely cover the space and assure you that the work is getting done the way you expect it to and you can reduce the amount of time you need to spend looking at this.*

Rita: *I'm still not clear.*

Tom: *Ok, let's walk through one. The first deliverable on the list is for me to provide a weekly status report for our VP. I pull together everything from the project managers, and you meet with us every week to review it and get corrections before we publish it. What are the things you are looking for so that I can do this before we meet, and eventually get* *good enough at it so that you don't need to review it?*

Rita: *Well, I will always want to review it before it is published, but it would be good if you would question these 3 things first so I don't have to keep asking the same questions all the time. (explains)*

Tom: *Great, I can do that. Also, you change the format every once in a while, and I can't see the pattern. What is it that makes you change the format so that I can just plan for that?*

Rita: *(laughs) I can see how that might look arbitrary, but there is a pattern to that. (explains)*

Tom: *Ok, so would you like me to build this schedule so we know what to do when?*

Rita: *That would be very helpful.*

Tom: *What else can I do that would take some of the day-to-day tasks from you?*

Rita: *Now that you mention it,…*

You can see this conversation was much more detailed and gave Tom the feedback he was looking for. Of course, the burden was on Tom to come prepared to the meeting, with specific questions. This conversation would have been a waste of time if Tom had gone into it with no preparation. As with any meeting, the best way to achieve the desired outcome is to know what you want before you start. Also, if you are the one asking the questions, you control the conversation. Prepare your questions ahead of time so that you can guide the conversation towards your desired outcome.

Let's talk about status reporting. It is a necessary evil. Your boss has a need to know whether the work is getting done. Either you can tell him, or he can ask you.

Both have their drawbacks. It's up to you to chose which option is more appropriate for your situation.

If you are telling him the status:

You continually give your boss a progress report so that he knows the current status at all times. You should have agreed ahead of time how often that progress needs to be reported and the mechanism for providing the status. Do you tell him once a week? When a step is completed? Or ad-hoc when you think of it? Also, should the status be provided verbally, in writing, or recorded somewhere? Most of the time, you will be providing status to your boss at a time when he is working on something else and not ready to pay attention. Hallway conversations will be forgotten, and emails will not be read and may even get lost.

If he is asking you for status:

If your boss has to ask you for status, that means he is usually preparing a report for his boss, or is worried about the current state of the project. He's in an emotional state and does not want to hear any explanation of why the work is not completed. Unless you can tell him with confidence the work is done, this conversation will not be pleasant.

The best path to providing a current status is to establish a location where it can be recorded and updated regularly. This location needs to be visible to your team and your boss, so that anyone can tell where you are just by looking. For complex projects and deliverables, this is usually recorded in a computer system. For something simple, an update to a chart or whiteboard on the wall may be sufficient. Of course, the boss may still ask for some supporting detail, but at least the overall status is readily available.

Here's an example of how Tom might address status with his boss:

Tom: *I also want to talk about status reporting. I'm thinking the best way to keep you informed about where I am is to build a calendar out on our shared drive with milestones for drafts, reviews, and final publication, and I can color code them so you can see at a glance where I stand. Would that work for you?*

Rita: *I like the idea, but I'm not sure that will give me enough details. How about we give it a shot and get back together in two weeks to review how well it's working?*

Here are some examples that have worked for others. Think creatively about how you can set up a system that will work for you.

- Staff with the responsibility of promoting an event sent out a daily report of ticket sales.
- Complex software development projects with a set of published milestones, updated in an online system weekly with a red/yellow/green status flag.
- An employee working on a complex problem with 5 stages to complete, each updated on her whiteboard at the end of the day.
- A chalkboard in the break room with the number of

widgets sold.

- A chart showing the funding raised against the goal.
- A spreadsheet showing houses vacant, rent collected, rent due.

In each case, the information shared is just enough to determine if the work is on track. Any deviation from the expected progress will require a more detailed explanation and discussion on how to correct it.

Which brings us to the last point: your boss will only be able to "turn his back" if he knows that you will raise issues to his attention. No one likes surprises, especially when the problem is left unaddressed so long that it becomes a crisis. Your job is to identify issues that are preventing you from completing your work, and to ask for the help you need. Even if you are able to resolve the problem by yourself, let your boss know if it will impact the timeline. If you can't resolve it by yourself, figure out who or what you need and ask for it. Get the right people involved as quickly as possible so that you can get past the problem.

There is a time in the life of every problem when it is big enough to see, yet small enough to solve.

~Mike Leavitt

Chapter 2: Every 2 Weeks We're Square

"It is our choices, Harry, that show us what we truly are, far more than our abilities."

— J.K. Rowling, Harry Potter and the Chamber of Secrets

Entitlement [From Wikipedia, the free encyclopedia]

In a casual sense, the term "entitlement" refers to a notion or belief that one (or oneself) is deserving of some particular reward or benefit.

Entitlement may also refer to the idea of an entitlement society, in which everyone receives the same or similar rewards, regardless of education, effort, and willingness to take risk.

You are not entitled. You were hired to do a job, and as long as you do that job you get paid. That's it. If you get paid every two weeks, then every two weeks you're square. When you were hired, you had an agreement of the roles and responsibilities you would take on, and in return you would be paid an agreed-upon sum of money. As long as you are fulfilling your end of that contract, you get paid. End of story.

In today's marketplace, we know that employees leave when they find another job that appears to offer more: more money, more challenge, more fun, more something. In a study conducted by the Bureau of Labor Statistics, 10,000 individuals were first interviewed in 1979 when they were between 14 and 22 years old. By 2010, members of that group had held 10.8 jobs per person, on average.

On the other hand, companies no longer hire for life either. The days of joining one company, working hard for 20 years or more, and then getting a gold watch and pension fund for retirement are over. Company layoffs are a reality, and most successful organizations are focused on profitability. As an employee, you are an expense, one of the largest expense line items, and therefore a line item that is closely monitored.

There is a balance that must be achieved between contribution to results and compensation.

If you want more compensation, you must first determine exactly what is needed to improve the organization's results and increase your contributions in that space.

Results Matter

Results are the only thing that matters. Your results, inasmuch as they contribute to the organization's results, will dictate your worth to the company.

Contribution

Compensation

Doing the job you were hired to do means you are continuing to deliver the same results. Even if you are content with the compensation you are receiving, this is a dangerous position. Today's marketplace dictates that companies continue to evolve and change. What you are doing today may no longer be important tomorrow, and you will no longer be performing a function necessary to the survival of the company.

For a company to continue to stay in business, each employee's contributions to the bottom line must outweigh the expense of keeping him or her on staff. Consider how much you cost the company, not just in salary but also in benefits, taxes, equipment, etc. Do your activities help the company make at least that much in revenue? Now, some positions are not directly responsible for revenue, but they do free up key resources to focus on revenue-generating activities. One of the very first hires a small business owner often makes is for an assistant to offload administrative tasks so the business owner can focus on bringing in new business. That assistant may not contribute to the bottom line, but will perform critical functions to keep the business running that frees up someone else to generate revenue.

Activity is Not Progress

Are you putting your efforts into the right activities that will bring about real progress? If you are constantly "working on" or "getting ready to" do something, and don't actually "put it in the done pile," you are not achieving results. So many projects stay at 95% complete for weeks and weeks and languish there. If you don't get it done, it doesn't count. No excuses.

As Stephen Covey says, "Begin with the end in mind." What is the target you are working towards? If you are not clear on how an activity contributes towards the goal, reevaluate whether you should be working on it. At the end of the day when you can say, "I've got a lot done today," make sure those items that you completed were the right items that help you achieve real results.

Watch the things that are keeping you busy every day, and ask yourself how these activities are helping you achieve something worthwhile. Meetings, email, conversations, internet research and hallway conversations can make you look busy but don't contribute to results. (We'll address more of this in Chapter 11.)

You are Not Entitled

So why is it that so many employees think they are entitled to more? That they can do the same thing day after day and just by nature of their existence warrant a higher salary, more perks or a promotion?

There are generally two categories of entitlement attitude that need to be addressed:

1. Elitism
2. Existence

Elitism

Entitlement due to elitism is generally a perception that you are somehow better than the average person based on external circumstances rather than personal achievement.

e•lit•ism or é•lit•ism n. [http://www.thefreedictionary.com]

1. The belief that certain persons or members of certain classes or groups deserve favored treatment by virtue of their perceived superiority, as in intellect, social status, or financial resources.

2.a. The sense of entitlement enjoyed by such a group or class.

b. Control, rule, or domination by such a group or class.

Consider this example:

A large Information Technology (IT) company changed its policy so that it would no longer hire entry level staff from the various local colleges. Instead, the company decided to select a handful of colleges where they would focus their recruiting efforts. These were colleges that were considered to be the "cream of the crop." What the company found was that the graduates from these colleges expected to be given higher salaries and positions of authority than those graduates they had recruited elsewhere. The recruits had no practical experience to offer, but just because they went to a "better" school the new staff members considered themselves entitled. One such hire insisted that he was not a mere computer programmer, he was a system architect. Never mind that he had never architected any computer system other than class assignments! The environment he was working in was an order of magnitude more complex than anything he had ever experienced in his academic career, but he felt that he was qualified for the job because of his degree and the institution from which he had earned it.

An employee with an elitism attitude will consider certain tasks beneath him. If you find yourself asking, "Why do I have to do that?" the next time your boss asks you to do something, carefully consider your motives. It's not your job? Every team member has the responsibility to make sure that every task required for success of the goal gets done. If the task is not your job, but the job needs to be done and you have the ability to do it, then do it. If a restaurant closes at 9 p.m. and the person who is supposed to wipe down the tables is busy cleaning up a mess elsewhere, you can either stand around and do nothing or pitch in and help. If you do nothing, you can be assured that is the level of support you will get from your teammates later when you need their help.

One of the signs of an effective team is that every member of the team pitches in to help the others when it is needed in order to complete the current block of work on time. A good working team has all of the team members focusing on a shared goal, not on boundaries between the individual roles and responsibilities. No one person's work is more or less important than the other's. Everyone has a vested interest in achieving the goal and will do whatever it takes to get there. If that means pitching in to help another team member with their assigned tasks, do it.

Existence

Entitlement due to existence occurs when an employee feels like he deserves more simply because he's been around for a little while. This occurs most often when the job market is growing, when employees have the option to find another position quickly. It can border on a subtle form of extortion, where the employee is demanding an increase in pay or they will leave.

For example:

A firm built up a division in India at the time the market there was very hot. What they found was that employees in India expected a pay raise and promotion after six months or they jumped ship to another company. These employees were not concerned with the contribution side of the equation, just the compensation. They expected to be rewarded simply for showing up for six months. These were employees that did not understand the industry the company was in, and used geography and time zone differences as an excuse why they could not learn it. Because the company was building its presence in India in an effort to cut labor costs, they were faced with the dilemma of continuing to hire new people or increasing salaries for existing employees to stabilize the labor force. Either choice would end up costing the company money, which would defeat the purpose of moving to India to cut costs.

In a depressed labor market, where jobs are harder to come by, the employee is more motivated to keep his job and does not usually use this tactic and threaten to leave. However, we do still see employees that continue to do the same job, with the same results, yet expect to be paid more simply because they've been there for a length of time. If they have not grown in knowledge, expertise and contributions, then there is no reason to expect a salary increase.

There's a story of a man who worked in sales for 15 years, continuing to use the same techniques over and over for his tenure. He claimed to have 15 years of sales experience, but in reality what he had was 1 year of sales experience repeated 15 times. If you truly want to earn more, you need to grow more. By increasing your knowledge and your value to the company, you are in a much better position for increased compensation.

Chapter 3: Use Your Own Brain; Mine's Busy

"When I say do your best, I mean your very best. You are capable of so much more."

— Gordon B. Hinckley

Entrepreneurs know that the way to attract customers is to serve them by solving their problems. The larger the problems you can solve for them, the more customers are willing to pay for their services. For example, look at the food industry. If a customer is hungry and just wants something to eat quickly, his choice is either a food cart on the street, a fast food drive-through, or a take-out counter. In all cases, the food is a commodity, just something to address his hunger quickly. He has to go get the meal, eat out of a paper bag or box, provide his own location to consume the meal, and clean up after himself. He will likely pay only a few dollars for his meal. Contrast that with a customer who wants to take clients out for a fine meal to impress them. He will look for an upscale restaurant with quality food, great service, and the right ambiance. He is looking for a total experience that will meet his needs, and he is willing to pay a premium price for this.

As an employee, you have customers too. While your company may dictate the items for sale to external customers and how those items are delivered, you have total control over how you serve your boss and your coworkers. Try to determine what their needs are and how you can help solve their problems. Too often employees focus on the immediate stumbling blocks and not on the long-term solutions. If a man is hungry, he doesn't want to hear how the wholesaler's truck hasn't arrived yet. Likewise, when your boss needs an analysis completed, he doesn't want to know how difficult it's been to get an appointment with a key resource. To increase your worth, and your value to your organization, make sure you are focused on providing solutions, not excuses.

When you review the four scenarios below, make an honest assessment of how you would normally respond. Your answers will provide you with insights as to how well you are serving your team.

Situation 1: Your boss asks you for a status about a project you are working on.

Do you:

1. Ask him a handful of questions about what you are supposed to do

2. Provide him with a clear picture of where you are and when you expect to complete the assignment

3. List some of the issues you are facing and how you are addressing them

4. Brush him off and tell him you have it under control

If you chose #1:

Your boss is asking for a status, which means he expects that you've already begun the work and are clear on what you've been assigned to do. Asking questions at this stage indicates that you did not take the assignment seriously when it was first given to you. You must make sure you are clear from the beginning. If questions arise during the course of the work, ask them. Don't wait for your boss to ask you for a status.

If you chose #2:

Congratulations, you are owning your space. Not only can you clearly communicate your progress, you also have a plan to complete the work. After all, you cannot communicate when you will complete the assignment with any degree of accuracy unless you understand the work and what it will take to complete it.

If you chose #3:

While your boss might be a detail oriented person, what he is really asking you for is an answer for when the work will be done. An analytical type of person might be interested in hearing the details, but most times the boss just wants to hear the answer to two questions: Is it done or not? And if not, when will it be? Keep in mind that if there are issues preventing you from getting the work done, you should be surfacing those when they are identified, not when the boss comes asking.

If you chose #4:

This is taking the concept of owning your space too far. While every boss appreciates an employee that takes care of his responsibilities, he is still the boss. Chances are he has to answer to someone higher up in the organization, or to customers or even the Board of Directors. When your boss asks you for information, share it. His role is to make sure projects are being completed and the team is moving towards stated objectives. Your role is to support him, and part of the way you do that is by making sure he understands what your status is.

Situation 2: You meet with your boss to review your completed assignment.

What happens?

1. Your boss reviews it with you in detail and asks for clarifications on specific items

2. You ask your boss questions about how to address parts of the assignment

3. Your boss expresses frustration and tells you work that still needs to be completed

4. Your boss reviews and approves it

Years ago, a VP in a Telecommunications firm had a sign on his wall called "Completed Staff Work."

The premise of Completed Staff Work is that the boss should not need to answer questions. The description is:

> "Completed staff work is the study of a problem, and presentation of a solution, by a staff member, in such form that all that remains to be done on the part of the boss is to indicate approval or disapproval of the completed action." (Codner, 1943)

In other words, you should not present work to your boss until you are sure that it is 100% completed and ready to be signed and forwarded on. You should no longer have open questions or gaps in the work.

In many cases, your boss will only provide a cursory review of the work and then ask you a few questions. Here is where you need to look at the kinds of questions being asked. Chances are your boss did not read what you put in front of him and he is asking questions to determine whether you covered all the critical points. If this is the case, questions are fine. On the other hand, if your boss is asking questions that are pointing out gaps in your proposal, you still have work to do.

The monkey is squarely on your back. It is your responsibility to care for it. By bringing incomplete work to your boss, you are essentially asking to transfer care of that monkey from your back to his. A good boss will recognize this and prevent it from happening. However, an inexperienced boss may feel compelled to take that monkey, and he will resent you for it. You do not want to be seen as an employee who causes the boss to work harder, the exact opposite of what you want.

Situation 3: Your team is facing a challenge with a particular work assignment and holds a meeting to address it.

Do you:

1. Read email and work on something else since this really isn't your area of responsibility
2. Ask questions to find out who screwed up
3. Make statements about what should have been done
4. Volunteer ideas to figure out how the team can move

forward

Response #1:

You might be tempted to disengage yourself from the discussion if the problem is in an area where you have no expertise. There are two reasons why this is the wrong approach:

Your teammates will see you as someone who is not willing to pitch in and help when they need it.

Those who are closest to the problem often cannot see it. Often it is someone with a different perspective that can spark an idea leading to the solution.

Response #2:

Assigning blame is counter-productive. All humans make mistakes, and it is by learning from them that we grow. As one manager put it, "The only people who don't make mistakes are those who are not working hard enough." If the focus is on blaming someone for making a mistake, everyone on the team gets the message that "mistakes are bad" and they will be less likely to innovate and take risks. Also, nothing good comes from making a person feel bad about himself. It doesn't solve the problem at hand, and it introduces a new morale problem as well.

Response #3:

Anyone who makes statements about what should have been done is just showing off. When the focus is backwards, towards the past, you are not making progress. Likewise, you'll see the same negative results as outlined in the previous answer. Consider that you are all teammates, and the time to speak up about a better way to do something is when it is actually being done, not afterwards. Contribute your ideas when they can be of the most help. Which is more valuable, the quarterback who makes an adjustment to the play when they are on the field on Sunday afternoon, or the armchair quarterback who lists what should have been done when they rehash the game on Monday morning?

Response #4:

The best habit to get into is to ask questions that start with "how can I" or "how can we." How can we fix this? How can we get product XYZ completed? Focus the attention on the desired outcome, and solicit ideas to get there. Again, results are what count. It doesn't matter what was done before; what matters is getting to the result. The moment you recognize that there is some problem or obstacle to be resolved before the team can achieve their objectives, start working on the solution. If you don't have the expertise, bring someone in that does. Problems don't generally go away by themselves, and left unattended they tend to grow. The best approach is to tackle it head on as soon as you recognize that it exists.

Situation 4: Your work is done and you have some quiet time.

Do you:

1. Surf the internet, take care of personal items, or cut out early and go home
2. Take a training course
3. Volunteer to help a coworker with their project
4. Work on a new idea or solution to a problem that no one is addressing

Any of the above can be the right answer or not, depending on the circumstances. Most people, when asked this question, will react to answer #1 as if it were a bad choice. But consider this situation: you've been working non-stop for the past 2 weeks to get your project done. You've worked late into the night, spent the majority of your weekend in the office, and now you're finally done. In this situation, can you see how it would be the right answer for you to go take care of the personal items you neglected on the weekend and go home? Work can come in cycles where you have to push yourself very hard for a period of time, and you must replenish yourself afterwards. Those who don't do this are those that suffer from job burnout.

Taking a training course or learning a new skill is a valuable exercise. The more you grow your skills, the more you are able to contribute. Just make sure the skills are you learning are those that are relevant to your job.

We've already talked about how important it is to help the team to achieve shared goals. If you have completed your part of the project, but someone else is lagging behind, pitch in. Here the caveat is to pitch in when you have the ability to help and not hinder progress. Well-intentioned coworkers who take on tasks they are not qualified to perform will usually just cause re-work later. Be honest about your abilities and use them to the team's best advantage.

There are a growing number of companies that have begun to recognize that the greatest innovations come from giving employees space to play around. If you've got some free time, look for ways to improve your products or processes at work. Google's gmail product was an invention of an employee looking for a better way for coworkers to communicate internally. What kinds of creative solutions can you dream up?

Part A: Action Plan

1. Understand the major revenue-generating activities for your company and how you contribute to them.

2. Document the list of expectations for your job and review with your boss.

3. Ask for and offer help when problems arise.

4. Standardize a process for communicating project status with your team and your boss.

5. For each project, establish criteria for completion.

Part B: Own Your Space

Chapter 4: How to Own Your Space So Everyone Knows it's Yours

You have to decide what your highest priorities are and have the courage — pleasantly, smilingly, non-apologetically, to say "no" to other things. And the way you do that is by having a bigger "yes" burning inside. The enemy of the "best" is often the "good."

— Stephen R. Covey

What Do You Want?

You have to define your space, clearly and intentionally. First and foremost, you have to decide what it is that you want. Stake your claim.

The job market has become like a game of musical chairs, where an employee is laid off from one position and is happy to land a job anywhere to stay employed. If the employee is not suited for that position, before long he will be back in the cycle of getting laid off and looking for his next job. This cycle is stressful and costly for everyone involved.

Define larger, long-term goals for your career and your life overall. Understand where you are headed and what you need to do to get there. Once you can link the day-to-day "have to" list with your long-term goals, you suddenly "want to" accomplish the things on your list. Without that larger perspective, it is hard to be inspired by the daily activities that you need to do. For example, a person who is interested in becoming a real estate investor might start by doing research on properties for someone else who is already successful in the field. While this task can become repetitive and mundane if looked at by itself, it becomes an important stepping stone in context of the larger career goal. When you start looking at your "to do" list and dreading some of the items on there, consider how these tasks fit into your aspirations, and they might not seem so dreadful after all.

Attitude

Do you have a victim's attitude or an owner's attitude? Most people, when asked that question, would automatically claim to be an owner. After all, who wants to be a victim? The unfortunate truth is that the majority of the working population has a victim's attitude.

Let's start with some definitions.

To own something is to have power or mastery over it. The owner controls the outcome, good or bad. On the other hand, a victim is one who has relinquished control to some outside force.

vic·tim [vik-tim] *n.* [http://dictionary.reference.com]

1. a person who suffers from a destructive or injurious action or agency: a victim of an automobile accident.

2. a person who is deceived or cheated, as by his or her own emotions or ignorance, by the dishonesty of others, or by some impersonal agency: a victim of misplaced confidence; the victim of a swindler; a victim of an optical illusion.

3. a person or animal sacrificed or regarded as sacrificed: war victims.

4. a living creature sacrificed in religious rites.

Invariably something will go wrong, and this is where the true test of your ownership will come. An owner will take responsibility for the problem and look for solutions. He will also spend time reflecting on how he could have prevented the failure and what lessons he can learn for the future.

A victim will make claims as to how the economy just isn't good, or the boss is an idiot, or someone else hasn't done his job properly. The moment you start to lay blame, you have put yourself into the role of the victim. It isn't your fault that the project failed, it's the economy, or your boss, or your coworker, or the phase of the moon. You've given up control to someone or something else.

Rob was a seasoned employee whose responsibility it was to gather key metrics for the department and publish them weekly. He'd been in this role for many years and had built key relationships throughout the company that enabled him to get access to the data he needed. He was very talented at synthesizing the information and putting it in a format that was easily understood by all levels of management. Everyone relied on his data and trusted him, knowing that he put in the due diligence to ensure that every metric was accurate. Everything was functioning like clockwork, until the company reorganized. Now Rob found himself with a new manager and a new director. The department strategies were shifted, and the teams were working to readjust to the new priorities. Except Rob, that is. He was waiting for his boss to tell him what to do. He claimed, "I'm not sure what metrics they want so I'm waiting for them to tell me." Unfortunately, neither the first nor second level management saw his reporting as a priority since they were engulfed in working through changes in the organization. So Rob just waited.

If you'd asked Rob, he'd deny having a victim's attitude but that is what it was. He was at the mercy of his management and lack of direction from them.

Let's look at this from the manager's point of view. To him, Rob was an employee on his staff that wasn't producing. He had performed the same function for a long time, but when the organization shifted Rob's lack of ownership become visible. The new manager did not see Rob as a talented member of the team with key business relationships that were already cultivated and at this disposal. He saw Rob as someone that was a problem.

Fortunately, Rob was given some coaching by another manager in the department that recognized the situation and had an owner's attitude. She advised him to brainstorm with his key business partners and come up with a proposal that he could present to his boss. After all, his boss was new and did not have access to the wealth of knowledge that Rob did. There was no reason why Rob needed to wait for his boss to tell him what to do. The result was that Rob collaborated with his stakeholders, built a prototype of a new dashboard that provided the information needed for the strategic direction of the department, and delighted his boss. He was no longer a victim, but a master of his domain.

Another dimension of an owner's attitude is facing reality. Acknowledge the signs that all is not rosy and adjust. You can read in the news of companies that face catastrophe because they failed to adjust their strategy to market conditions. When you turn the blinders on, you are leaving your chances for success up to fate.

One manager started to recognize signs that his team was getting bored. They provided an important function for their customers, but it was the same every time with little variation. Adding to the problem was that the team no longer received any recognition for what they did. They had performed this function successfully for so long that it was expected of them. Absenteeism started to increase, the level of joking and camaraderie of his team had dropped off, and finally one of the key employees left for another position. The manager knew he needed to find a way to reenergize his team quickly. He studied the industry and the strategic direction of the company and recognized a new trend that they could capitalize on with almost no increase in cost. His team was delighted and the company introduced a new service for their customers that differentiated them from their competition.

You can do the same for yourself. If you find your attitude slipping, or you are getting bored with your work, ask yourself what you can do to change your situation. Don't wait for someone else to do it for you.

Motivation and Momentum

Your coworker comes to you and says, "I just can't seem to get motivated today." Or perhaps it is you who realizes you have no motivation. What happens next? For most people, the answer is very little. They allow themselves to drift through the day, watching the clock until it's time to go home. They see motivation as something they need to "get" before they can get on with whatever it is they are supposed to be doing. Lack of motivation becomes a state of reality that gives them the excuse to procrastinate.

Motivation comes from within you. It is an internal state that activates behavior and directs you toward a goal. You cannot be motivated by someone else, just as you cannot motivate others. To be motivated means that you have a desire to do what is necessary to achieve a future goal. If we break this down, you'll see that there are several factors that must be true before you can be motivated:

- You must have a vision of a future goal. If you are not striving towards something, you will not be motivated to get anything done.

- You must see that vision as a desirable thing to achieve. If it doesn't *inspire* you, you won't *perspire* to achieve it.

- You must believe that the goal is achievable. Lack of belief holds more people back than any other factor.

- You must be clear on what you are working to achieve. Have a clear vision of the goal.

- You must be able to lay out specific actions you can take

to get you closer to the goal. You may not be able to see all the steps at first, but you need to be able to take the first few. Travel down the road as far as you can see, and when you get there you'll find that you can see further.

There are also several killers of motivation to watch out for. The most disastrous is routine, or lack of challenge. You must challenge yourself to do something new or learn something new. Otherwise you'll find yourself just going through the motions, like a hamster on a wheel. Sales people hear the same objections over and over in their jobs. To combat boredom, they will often script multiple responses to those objections and try new ones all the time. A team responsible for producing the same report week after week found new ways to automate the process. What can you do in your job to challenge yourself or improve upon existing processes?

Another killer of motivation is lack of clarity, whether that is lack of direction or confusion over the direction. One of the conditions for motivation is a clear vision on what you are working to achieve. Remove all signs of confusion by continuing to ask questions and brainstorm ideas until you have a good sense of what the future can look like.

Weak is he who permits his thoughts to control his actions; strong is he who forces his actions to control his thoughts.

-Og Mandino

High achievers know that it is what you do every day that

dictates your success. It doesn't matter what your level of motivation is; what matters is what you do. Rather than waiting for motivation to magically arrive and inspire you to take action, put systems in place that force you to take action every day. What is the one thing you continue to procrastinate, even though you know you must do it to be successful? Perhaps it is making phone calls to prospective customers or finishing the book you are working on. Whatever it is, schedule activities in your day to work on these items. Whether you feel like it or not, take action. You'll find that the action will drive your motivation, not the other way around.

When you are stuck, take bold, massive action and do it quickly. When you feel your momentum slowing down, you are letting doubts start to sink in. Push past these doubts with action, and increased action will help you build confidence. It's been said, "Motion overcomes emotion."

It all begins with a decision. Decide to begin today. That decision will drive action, action builds momentum, and momentum builds the desire for increased action. Before you know it, you'll be well on the road toward achieving your goals.

Initiative

If you work in an environment where you understand the

goals of the company and your role in contributing towards those goals, you are one step ahead. Most employees don't have this insight. Maybe they weren't listening when the boss explained it to them, or they have a boss that assumed they knew this already and never talked about it with them directly. If you don't know, it is up to you to find out. In small companies, your boss's goals are likely the same as the company goals. However, in very large corporations the company goal is broken down layer-by-layer, into smaller sub-goals for each department. As discussed earlier, your performance is measured in terms of contribution to the company goals. Ask questions until you are 100% clear on what you should be doing to support them.

Now that you understand what to do, it's time to take initiative and go do it. Oncken and Wass, in an article published in the *Harvard Business Review*, 1974, outline 5 degrees of initiative (William Oncken, 1974):

1. Wait until told what to do
2. Ask what to do
3. Recommend, then take resulting action
4. Act, but advise at once
5. Act on own, routinely report

You can be at different levels of initiative depending on the work and the work environment. Here is an explanation of each of the levels:

Waits until told what to do

This is the most frustrating of employees, the one that is content to stand around and do nothing until someone tells them what to do. They are essentially a body without a head, which then requires someone else to use part of their head governing the daily actions of this employee. Unless you are a brand new employee who has not yet been told what their responsibilities are, you should never be this person.

Asks you what they should do

This employee recognizes that she was hired for a reason and it was not to be idle. She doesn't know what to do but will ask for direction. The benefit of this self-identification is that the boss now knows he has some capacity within his team that he is underutilizing and can take steps to correct it. When you are in an unfamiliar situation and don't know the overall distribution of responsibility, it is appropriate to ask what to do. Generally this is the result of a poor manager who has not laid out the team's roles and responsibilities to the point where each team member knows who is supposed to do what. The result is the team members cannot take independent action without fear of infringing on someone else's area of responsibility.

Recommends what should happen, then does it

Employees in this category understand the situation and will recommend a course of action. He will then act, based upon approval of that recommendation. An employee with low confidence about the work at hand will seek this approval, just as those who are in an environment where the boss insists on reviewing everything first will want to receive this approval as well.

Does it, but tells you first

This is the employee that knows what needs to be done and just does it, but tells his boss right away so as to avoid any surprises. Employees in this category generally take the approach that "it's easier to get forgiveness later than to get permission first." There are bosses who insist on knowing everything their team is doing so that they can answer questions from those higher up without losing face. If you have a boss that has a high need for control, tell him what you are doing. If someone approaches your boss to ask about the project you are working on and he is unaware, you can be guaranteed he will not be happy with you.

Acts independently, keeps you informed

This is the highest degree of autonomy that we all strive for at work. Keep in mind, though, that to achieve this level you must first earn your freedom, as outlined earlier. When your boss trusts you and recognizes that you have your area of responsibility under control, you will be in a position to act where you see best and just report status regularly.

The progression through the degrees of initiative is both a factor of your behavior and your boss's confidence in you. Keep in mind that some bosses have not reached a level of maturity where they are able to trust their employees without micro-managing. Before you write it all off as your manager's fault, though, take a hard look at where you are in this spectrum. Your behavior will influence how others treat you. If you are continuously being proactive and taking the correct steps towards achieving the stated goals, open a conversation with your boss so that he is aware of the progress you are making and increase his level of confidence in you.

The Power of 5 is a concept from Jack Canfield's The Success Principles™ How to Get from Where You Are to

Make Your Job Great

57

Where You Want to Be. The concept is simple: every day take 5 actions that take you closer to your goal. This is all about taking action, but doing it in such a way that is not overwhelming. So many projects never get off the ground because they seem too large and intimidating. Find 5 things you can do that will move you forward, do this every day, and you will be amazed at how much you can accomplish. Just starting things going by doing a simple task leads to bigger and stronger momentum. As the proverb says, "Well begun is half done."

Take the time every night to write down your 5 things for the next day. This accomplishes 2 things: it gives your subconscious all night to work on the problem, and it also allows you to hit the day running when you wake up in the morning. Try it for a week and see how it feels.

Look for the White Space

A VP of a large corporation shared her strategy for success, and it was simply to "look for the white space." The culture in her company often pitted the executives against each other, where multiple departments would race to complete a project and the first one done, wins. While others around her were vying for the same handful of "hot" projects, she took a different path. She would often look for initiatives that would support these "hot" projects that were not being addressed. For example, while her colleagues rushed to complete a new billing initiative, she focused on customer adoption. While all the focus was on her colleagues and their departments during the early phases of the product lifecycle, she became the hero of the story when she stepped in with a solution to a problem raised in one of the latter phases.

There is always white space in every job, areas that are not being addressed or are fuddled through without a solid plan. There are always problems that need to be addressed. Be the person that looks for these opportunities and finds the solutions before they become critical stumbling blocks to the organization.

Always remember you are a unique individual with unique talents and strengths. You are not serving yourself or your organization by following along with what everyone else is doing. Look at ways to contribute to the goals of the company that capitalize on your individual strengths.

Chapter 5: How to Communicate to Get What You Want

*If you can't explain it to a six year old,
you don't understand it yourself."*

— Albert Einstein

Before you can ask for what you want, you have to know what that is. It is up to you to identify your career goals and seek out your manager and other mentors within the company that can help you identify job assignments that will stretch your capabilities toward the goals you've established.

What are the aspects of your job that you enjoy the most? You want to identify the roles that you perform today that you get the most satisfaction from. Maybe there is a particular activity that gets you so absorbed that you lose all track of time, or a situation that energizes you. Find out what those things are, and then ask for more of them. On the flip side, figure out what parts of your job drain you, things that you have to drag yourself to do, and see if there is a way to do less of those activities.

Tony was a project manager in a large corporation and he hated his job. He was put in this role after a corporate reorganization, and he was not suited for it. He did not like running the meetings, managing the project plan, and chasing the team to get their status. The result was that he was not very good at it either. His team did not have a manager for some time after the reorganization, so he floundered. A new manager was hired, and he stunned them all by asking them each to describe the part of their job that they liked the best and the least, and the last time they felt appreciated for what they did. No one had ever asked those questions before. As Tony thought about it, he realized that the one thing he loved was training new employees. He loved everything about it: walking them through the steps, explaining the tools, and answering their questions as they struggled with their first few projects. At the time, the department itself was in disarray, with little standardization of process from one project manager to the next. To his delight, Tony was enlisted to document a standard process and train the entire team.

Without the introspection encouraged by Tony's new manager, he would have become one of those employees that just drifted through his days, miserable, until he quit or got fired. In his situation, it was a company reorganization that cast him in a role where he was incompetent, not a job change of his choosing. For many others, promotions can have the same results. Make sure you identify the kinds of activities that energize you and those that sap your energy. Seek out opportunities to do more of those that energize you and less of those that don't. It's that simple.

Mindreading

No one knows what you want until you tell them. Don't assume they can read your mind or automatically know what is important to you. Tell them.

Anna was a star employee who had been identified as having management potential. Her boss started to groom her for promotion, giving her assignments that required her to get work done by directing the efforts of others. To his delight, she excelled. The work was done perfectly, with no tradeoff between quality and schedule. Those working with her respected her, and fully expected to see her promoted into management. Imagine the surprise of her boss and her coworkers when she turned it down. She told him bluntly, "I don't want your job." Why? Anna knew that she had the potential to be a good manager, but she also knew she could not do it justice with the point she was at in her life at the time. Her children were very young and her husband had medical issues that gave him great pain and made it difficult to move around. Anna's priority was her family, and she had established a schedule that allowed her to balance her work and her home life with the job that she currently had. She knew the management in her company were under a great deal of stress and worked long hours, something she was not willing or able to do. Shortly thereafter, she left the company to take another position that allowed her to work from home part time and gave her more flexibility in working hours.

Things might have turned out differently if Anna and her boss had had an open communication about her personal situation and career aspirations. Instead, she put her boss in a position where he looked foolish, sponsoring her for promotion when she was unwilling to accept the position. No one likes this kind of surprise. Anna might have landed in a better position in her new job, but the company she left lost a considerable amount of knowledge and expertise with her departure.

If your boss does not ask you what you want, tell him anyway. Too often managers make the assumption that everyone is like them and wants the same thing they do. Go through the exercise of identifying what you like to do, what you don't like to do, and job assignments that you'd like to experience. Be as specific as possible so that your team can help you. Remember, chances are the very things that you don't like to do are things that others enjoy.

Lack of Clarity

Mixed messages cause paralysis. As witnessed in the following exercise, giving someone conflicting directions just causes confusion and you will not receive the results you want.

A group of 15 women was asked to participate in an exercise using the kid's game where one person was to seek out a target based on whether the rest of the group shouted out "warmer," "hotter," "burning hot" as the person moved closer to the goal, and "cold," "colder," "freezing cold" as she moved away from it. In this exercise, the volunteer was not told what the target was, and the rest of the group was handed a card indicating the target. What they didn't know was that there were two targets on opposite sides of the room. When the volunteer began to move, half the room shouted "colder" while the other half shouted "warmer." After only 2 or 3 steps, the volunteer stopped moving. No matter which way she turned half the room told her she was wrong, so she became paralyzed.

(As an interesting side-note, when this same exercise was repeated with young children, the volunteer did not become paralyzed. Instead, she began running in circles around the room, clearly leaving the chaos behind to focus on something that brought her joy.)

Your communication must be clear.

Communication fails if the listener does not hear the same message that you intended to say. Understand that there are two sides of every communication: the sender and the receiver. Both have their own circumstances, experiences, beliefs, and objectives that can distort the message and lead to misunderstandings. For example, consider a single mother with a full-time job whose boss announces that the company has just signed a large contract that would bring in a significant amount of revenue. She might interpret that to mean that she will have to work longer hours and enlist the help of her mother to care for her children. Her coworker, a woman with less family pressures and highly motivated by achievement, might see this as a huge opportunity to do something new and exciting. Both women heard the same words, but the message they internalized was very different. Every person is tuned to the same radio station: WIIFM (What's In It For Me). They filter messages based on how they perceive the new information to impact them and those they care about. Keep this in mind when you interact with others, and help them see how the information applies to them.

It's your job to get your message across clearly.

The listener will interpret what you say in his own way, so it is up to you to make sure your point is coming across loud and clear. How closely someone listens depends on self-interest, who the messenger is, and how they deliver the message. Follow these guidelines:

Know what you want to say.

As with all interactions, have an outcome in mind. What is the message you want the listeners to walk away with? Take the time to get your thoughts in order before you speak, and focus on just a few key points. Don't dilute your message by overcommunicating.

Establish credibility.

If you don't already have a relationship with the people you are speaking to, they will be wondering why they should listen to you. If you do already have a relationship, the listener will filter your message based on what they know about you. Before jumping right into the point you want to make, spend a bit of time *positioning* yourself as a knowledgable expert. What experience have you had with this topic? Can you cite examples of previous successes? Have you done considerable research in this area? Set the stage so that your audience quits wondering why they should listen to you and instead focuses on your message.

Get to the point.

Two men were offering a training course on a marketing subject where they had a considerable amount of expertise and the audience was anxious to hear what they had to say. Unfortunately, they spent the first 20 minutes working with the broadcasting technology, deciding who was going to say what, and talking about their backgrounds. By the time they were ready to teach the subject matter, the audience had lost interest. The presenters were unprepared and that made them look unprofessional.

Speak slowly and clearly.

Pause and take a breath. Have you ever heard a novice speaker who was so nervous it seemed like he plowed through the entire presentation in one continuous burst of words? Instead of listening to his words, you find yourself fascinated with his breathing and wondering when he will take his next breath. Also, remember that there may be people in your audience for whom your language is not their native tongue, or perhaps they come from a location where the speech patterns are slower than yours. You must speak slowly to be understood.

Use words the listener will understand.

This is not the time to show off your knowledge of vocabulary. Using unfamiliar words or those that require specialized knowledge the audience does not have only serves to make you look arrogant and does nothing for your message. You will lose your listeners. If they are struggling to understand something you just said, they will stop and think about it. At that point anything else you say goes unheard because they have just turned inward and are no longer listening. You also run the risk of angering your audience. No one wants to be made to feel like they are not as smart or as competent as you. They get angry because you make them look bad. Neither is a good option if your intent is to share a message.

Use examples, stories, or diagrams to illustrate your point.

If your words are not 100% clear, stories or examples can

help explain what you are trying to say. You've heard the expression that a picture is worth a thousand words. We tend to think in pictures so help the listeners understand better by providing those pictures, either in words or in actual visual images.

Ask the listener to repeat it back.

Confirm that the listener heard what you intended to say by having them repeat it back to you in their own words. A good way to do this is to ask for the listener to provide an example or to recap the key points at the end of the meeting.

Ask questions to confirm understanding.

For example, if you've just given an intern an assignment, ask them to describe for you how they plan to tackle the assignment. This gets them to use their words instead of yours and will demonstrate for you how well they understood the assignment.

Have you ever been in a situation when you walked away from a conversation and asked someone if they had any idea what that person was talking about? It happens more often than you think. Maybe the listener didn't want to admit ignorance of a certain subject by asking a question, or maybe he did ask and got a convoluted answer that did nothing to clarify the situation.

A good practice to get into is to use more than one form of communication. You might explain the task at hand in a conference call with the team, and then follow it up with an email outlining the steps in writing. Better yet, ask someone who listened to the call to document the steps and distribute it.

You'll be surprised how often the words you say are not fully understood by those listening.

A small business owner had hired a consulting team in India to build an application for him. He was continually frustrated that the work delivered by the team was never quite what he asked for. By following the simple advice of asking them to send back an email outlining what he'd asked them to do, he found that he was not being clear enough in his specifications. It's much cheaper and easier to fix the specifications at this point then after the product is delivered.

Time and Place

When you want to communicate, pay attention to what else is going on around you. Make sure you have the focus and attention you need for your audience to hear your message. One public speaker tells the story of a corporate event being held right before Christmas where he was asked to provide training on sales techniques. However, right before he was scheduled to talk, the Sales VP announced that there would be no bonuses paid out that year. There was absolutely nothing that speaker could do or say to regain the audience's attention after that!

If you want to have a conversation with your boss about your job, don't just stop him in the hallway with the question "do you have a minute?" Schedule it so that he is not distracted by some other activity. What you have to say is important and should be allocated sufficient time on both your calendar and his.

Consider the environment. Can you talk about the issue in the hallway, on the phone, over lunch, or do you need to go into a conference room and close the door? Do you need to share materials or is a verbal conversation all that is needed? Can you just send an email? Pay careful attention to the environment so that the message you need to communicate can be heard.

Three Types of Information Processing Preferences

How we take in and remember new information is one of the basic principles of the study of Neuro-Linguistic Programming (NLP). NLP is the relationship between how we think (neuro), how we communicate (linguistic) and how we behave (programming). We use our five senses to process information about the world around us, but each of us predominately uses one of three senses:

- Audio (sound)
- Visual (sight)
- Kinesthetic (touch)

We can see information in pictures, feel it kinesthetically, or hear it as sounds. You can tell which sense you resonate with the most by the words you use to describe the information pulled out of our brain.

A visual person would ask questions such as, "Is that clear?" or "Do you see what I'm saying?" Look for words like these:

- Make a scene
- Clear as a bell
- Take a look
- See eye-to-eye
- Bright future

- Plainly see
- Appears

An auditory person would ask, "How does that sound to you?" or "Let's discuss our options". Listen for these words:

- Ring a bell
- Loud and clear
- Call on
- Inquire
- To tell the truth
- Listen

A kinesthetic person uses, "Are you ready to get moving?" or "It all boils down to...". Here's the words you'd react to:

- Hang in there
- Grasp
- Smooth operator
- Handle it
- Slipped my mind
- Pull some strings

Listen to the words a person uses to identify their primary representational system. Keep in mind, we all use all three of these in varying degrees. With an individual, you need to identify the one that he uses the most and tailor your speech to use words that correlate to that system. You'll be "speaking the same language," a technique that will help you build rapport and communicate better. If your boss asks you to "get a grip on the situation" and you respond with "I'll take a look at it," you are not speaking the same language. Your boss will think you didn't take his request seriously and with the same sense of urgency. If instead you said something like, "I'll get right on it," you'd be speaking to him in the same representational system he used.

In a setting where you are presenting to a group of people, you obviously cannot single out any one style. Include key words and phrases for all three senses to appeal to the entire audience. Each person will "hear" the words directed at their primary representational system and think you are speaking directly to them. If there are key individuals in the audience that you want to be sure to persuade, try to single them out before the meeting to identify their primary sensory input mechanism, and then establish eye contact with each of them when you use the appropriate words in your presentation.

Four Major Personality Types

While we each have a distinct set of traits that makes us unique, studies have categorized four major personality types that we must consider in our communication styles. We have a tendency to talk to others in the same style that we like to receive information. To effectively communicate to everyone, you have to incorporate styles that will appeal to all four types.

The Analyzer:

- The Analyzer is detail oriented, analytical, and prefers to research the facts
- You cannot rush an analyzer into making a decision quickly and they will generally be immune to emotional triggers.
- When addressing the analyzer, provide facts and figures, and use handouts if possible.

The Director

- The Director is busy, impatient, results oriented, and respects credentials.
- This is the smallest percentage of the population, but the majority of these types are in positions of leadership.
- When speaking to Directors, have a tight outline and stick to the schedule. Speak with authority and use bullet points.

The Entertainer

- The Entertainer is everyone's best friend. He loves people and stories, and focuses on fun.
- Entertainers are emotional decision makers and will respond best to emotional persuastion techniques.
- To speak to Entertainers, include personal stories. If possible, meet them in advance and call them by name in your presentation.

The Supporter

- The Supporter focuses on affiliation and cooperation with others. Supporters prefer stability and structure.
- Supporters do not like to shake things up and will only shift their way of doing things when it is clear that it is best for the team.
- Use team examples and introduce new concepts gradually when speaking to Supporters.

Start by identifying which of these is your personality type, but BEWARE! Your natural inclination is to structure your communication style according to your type, which can be a disaster.

Phil was by nature an analyzer, who liked to thoroughly research the options before making a decision. He once had to present a recommendation to his CIO and failed miserably. As Phil started walking through Plan A and all the charts related to his research, the CIO impatiently said, "Got it." "Ok." "What's next?" Phil received the same response as he walked through Plan B. Looking at his watch, then pointedly at Phil's boss, the CIO asked, "What's the bottom line?"

Clearly the CIO was a Director. Phil's presentation would have succeeded had he spoken directly, started with "here's what we recommend" followed with a few key points of why that recommendation was chosen. By using an inappropriate style in this presentation, Phil was not able to convince the CIO to back his recommendation. Worse, the CIO now had an unfavorable impression of Phil and his abilities.

Whether you admit it or not, people form an impression of you based on your ability to communicate. You may be the smartest person on the team, but you must also know how to get your ideas across so that others notice. Beyond the basics of speaking or writing clearly, the study of interpersonal communication will provide you with advanced skills that will make you more effective.

Chapter 6: Simple Steps to Treat People Right So That They Are Happy to Work With You

No one cares how much you know until they know how much you care.

—Theodore Roosevelt

It's all about relationships. It doesn't matter if the company you work for is large or small, or if the people you need to work with are in your department or a different company altogether. People all have a common need, and that is to feel like they are special. Treat them right and they will be happy to work with you.

The world is split between people who prefer to work with people and those who prefer to work on tasks. You have to work with both regardless of your preference.

Those with a preference for working on tasks have to learn to spend some time focusing on people. If all you talk about is work, especially if you are the boss, you'll be seen as cold and uncaring. You might care deeply, but that won't come across. For your team to like you, want to work with you, and be loyal to you, you have to show them you care. Here are some powerful but simple techniques to help you do that.

Thank You

Other than the person's name, these are the most powerful words you can use. Look for ways to use them, over and over. One of the reasons most cited for why employees leave their jobs is because they feel under-appreciated. Too often we are quick to point out when something is not right, but neglect to acknowledge when it is. You don't have to be the boss to influence this. When someone does something that benefits you, say thank you. It's that simple. You don't need any special training, budget, or committee approval. Just say the words.

Have you ever heard of a situation where someone said thank you but the other person didn't hear it? This is very common. If you really want your gratitude to be heard (and felt), consider the words you use. We are so conditioned to say "thank you" or a simple "thanks" in certain situations that it often goes unnoticed. So even if you are saying it to your coworker, she still feels unappreciated because she didn't register the words. How do you combat this? Say it differently so that it interrupts the pattern. "Thanks a million" or "I want to thank you for" or "you really came through for me and I appreciate it" are words that will be heard where a perfunctory "thank you" will not.

Julie was asked to pull out all the stops to pull some budget information together for a big meeting the next day. To accomplish this, she had to work late into the night and enlist the help of a coworker in India to get it all done in time. She handed it off to her supervisor, who thanked her for it. At this point, Julie really didn't hear the thank you because all she was interested in was going home and getting some rest. Her boss went to the meeting, got the budget approved, and sought out Julie the next day. In that conversation, Julie's boss again thanked her for the work and shared the outcome with her. This time Julie heard the message and felt the appreciation from her boss.

> *Good communication is not just what you say; it's also what the recipient hears.*

In this situation, even though the boss had thanked Julie when she turned in the work, Julie didn't hear it. Her boss could have easily left it like that; after all she'd thanked her once. But her boss was insightful enough to know that her message had been lost and needed to be repeated. Remember, good communication is not just what you say; it's also what the recipient hears.

Get Personal

When you come to work, you don't leave the rest of your life at the door. You are a whole human being, and work is only one dimension in your life. Granted, when you are at work you should be engaged in activities to further the goals of the organization, but you must get personal to form relationships with your coworkers that will make you all more effective as a team. In a virtual environment, where your team is spread across locations and you are not able to see each other face to face, it is even more important to intentionally get personal. It's just a little bit harder. You can't go to lunch, or share a story over coffee, or put a little red stocking on someone's wall at Christmas time. You have to use the tools available to you.

Here are some examples:

Conference calls

While you are waiting for team members to join, strike up a conversation with those that are on the call early. Ask about their weekend, or share a story from yours. Find out what their plans are for summer vacation, and congratulate them on their first grandchild. Once the team is assembled, you can turn the conversation back to the agenda. A word of caution: don't get carried away! Get back to business as soon as the team is assembled.

Humor

Sometimes you just need to get silly. Keep it in good taste, of course, but make fun of something. Laughter is one of the best ways to break up tension. You'll have to use good judgment here, but humor can be very powerful. You'll be seen as someone fun to work with and people will like you more. Look for an opportunity to introduce some humor but keep it short, simple and tasteful.

An example: A salesperson spent weeks talking with a business owner to get him to buy his product, and the salesperson was absolutely convinced that his was the best solution. The business owner wasn't sure, and kept making references to "not drinking the Kool-Aid." Finally, at the end of a long presentation, the business owner agreed to buy the product. The salesperson promptly went and got a glass of water and presented the business owner with a packet of Kool-Aid mix from his pocket that he'd been carrying around just for this moment.

Photos

Put up photos of your team, either in a common location visible to everyone or on a virtual board. When your team is spread across the globe, they may never meet each other. Find a place for everyone to post their picture so that you can see what everyone looks like.

One word of advice: encourage personality. There is nothing more boring than a bunch of posed photos of a person sitting in an office. A rule I once used was: "no cubicles, no suits."

Birthday cards

With today's technology, it is so simple to send an e-card. Have the team post their birthdays with their photos and then use that to trigger an e-card on their birthday. It's a simple technique that gets noticed.

Anniversaries

Celebrate years of service at your staff meetings. Whether someone has been working there a year, 5 years, or 20, congratulate them.

Non-working meetings

If you are in a common location, you can plan to go to lunch together or to an off-site location for fun. If you don't have this luxury, at least once in a while plan a meeting where you don't talk about work. One team set up quarterly meetings where they just used the time to talk about what was going in in each other's lives and to talk about hobbies and special events.

Video conferencing

If you have the technology to do a video conference call, then use it. The majority of the population prefers visual input, and seeing each other while talking is much more natural. We often learn more about a person by watching body language and mannerisms. In today's global working environment, you may not ever get to meet your coworker in person. Using video conferencing, you have an opportunity to "see" him and get to know him a little better.

Diversity

Our world has flattened and it is common now to work with people from different cultures. Take the time to learn about each other. Ask a team member to describe one of their customs or go sample some food from their country. Use the internet technology to go look at the country where they live.

A caveat: Your coworkers are not your counselors. While it is perfectly okay to let others know of events happening in your life, don't take this too far. Keep it positive. Share the story of your son's award, but keep the discussion about how to cope with his drinking for your friends outside of work. We've all heard stories of coworkers who come to work complaining in gory detail about their ex-husband. You should be professional at all times, which means no gripe sessions, no emotional breakdowns, and certainly no outbursts of anger. We'll address this more in Chapter 8.

Relationships

Look for ways to form new relationships that are mutually beneficial. Seek out different people and get to know what they are working on, what their problems are, and what gets them excited to come to work in the morning. You may find that you have some common goal where you can join forces and help each other. Maybe you will think of another person you can introduce him to, or information you can share. Remember the old adage, "It's not what you know, it's who you know." While many say this cynically when passed up for a promotion, the truth is that you should continually cultivate relationships at work. The key to this is to be a giver, not a taker. Look for ways you can help them, not what they can do for you. If you can find a way to help each other at the same time, then everybody wins.

Glenn had a job to do that required him to work after hours so that he would have access to the resources he needed without being disruptive to the rest of the business. His job was to artificially stress these resources to the point of breaking so that they had a good understanding of the load they would take under normal conditions. To do this during business hours would slow down the work everyone else was doing and potentially stop them altogether once he hit the breaking point. His only option was to begin his day when everyone else was ending theirs. It was lonely work that put a strain on his health and took away all his time with his family. Then he found another solution. He realized that the department that manufactured these resources had a vested interest in knowing the outcome of his tests, and even better, they had another parallel installation all set up for them to build and test new features. Glenn partnered with this team so that they had access to his expertise, and he had access to their parallel environment to run his tests. He extended his tests to accommodate the needs of the developers and in doing so he had advance notice of all new features as well as direct input into their development. Best of all, he was able to perform all his testing during regular business hours and go home to his family at night.

In this story, Glenn found a way to build a relationship with a new group of people where both had something to gain. This was not accomplished by following normal chains of command in the company, but by having personal conversations with the lead technician in the other department. He'd met him once before on a business trip, but didn't really know much about him. To start the conversation, he invited him to meet in the cafeteria for coffee and talked to him about his family and his hobbies before ever really discussing work. Over time, the two men formed a friendship that served them both personally and professionally for many years.

Find a way to keep track of what you learned about each person you meet. Above all, remember names. You will be forgiven all kinds of memory lapses if you only remember this one thing. However, take the time to record everything you can about this person so that you don't forget. One salesman shares a story of how he won the business of a large firm simply by remembering where the owner went on vacation and inquiring about the trip afterwards.

Respect Boundaries

You're working on a hot project, staying at the office late into the night. Suddenly you realize that John has information that would help you with the next step. The problem is that it is 9:30 at night and John was home sick that day. Do you call him at home or wait until morning to see if he comes into work the next day?

Your teammate is on vacation and you can't find the meeting minutes from last week's staff meeting that he sent out. Do you call him? Or do you go to the staff meeting and ask someone else for the information?

Donna's young child was hospitalized and she has not been in the office for two days. Her coworker, Sai, is filling in for her. You don't know Sai at all, but you know Donna has been working with a particular customer that you have a meeting with. Who do you call, Donna or Sai?

Believe it or not, there are many people who get so caught up in what they are working on that they forget to consider personal boundaries. In their minds, their project is the most important and nothing else is relevant. None of the cases listed above are good reasons to call the employee at home. None of them. Yet there are those who would call without a passing thought.

You've got to realistically assess the importance of what you need against consideration for the other person's circumstances. If your burning need can wait until normal business hours, then do so. If there is no critical need that warrants an intrusion on someone's personal time, let it go. **Even if you really, really want to get it done now.**

We all juggle different aspects of our lives, from work to play to family to other pursuits. Respect that. If you overstep the boundaries when it is not appropriate, you will only end up with hard feelings from that coworker, and you'll likely get less of a response from that person the next time. Save your interruptions for those rare occasions when it truly can't be helped, and the person will respect you for it.

Show You Care

A team of software developers in Tampa, Florida were getting increasingly agitated one afternoon as their boss sat in his office with the door closed, oblivious to what was happening. The employees all had their computers tuned to the news stations as they heard more dire predictions about the huge storm that was bearing down on their area. No work was getting done as they speculated whether they should leave to stock up on supplies and get their kids out of school. The boss said and did nothing. Finally, one of the team leaders sent them all home and said she'd deal with the boss.

What message did the boss inadvertently send to his team that day? Did they "feel the love"? Absolutely not! His subordinates where griping about him, saying things like, "I can't believe he's just sitting in there." They saw him as cold an uncaring. While this was not at all true, the damage was done. In this particular situation, when the team leader approached the boss and told him what had happened, he was completely supportive of her decision. He agreed that the safety of his employees and their families was important, but he was so absorbed in his work that he failed to see what was happening. Unfortunately, this is something you can't undo.

You can have all the expertise in the world, but if your coworkers don't believe you care about them and the work you are doing, you will not get all of their cooperation and support. No one wants to work with the know-it-all that completes his part of the project and then walks away, without concern as to whether his teammates are struggling.

So how do you show you care? It's very simple if you honestly do care about them. Here are just a few examples:

- Listen when others are speaking. Really listen. Focus on them and what they are saying, not on the email you just got.
- Respond with the appropriate words or actions when they share events in their lives. Congratulate them on the new baby. Send a sympathy card when their favorite Uncle Tony passes away.
- Help them with a problem they are having. If you've conquered a particular problem before and know how to solve it, share it with your coworker. Don't leave them to suffer through it alone.
- Invite them to lunch - especially the new folks. They don't know anyone, haven't found their place in the team yet, and would very much appreciate an opportunity to have lunch with you.
- Let others know when you are going to get coffee and ask if anyone else wants one.
- Put in 100% of your effort to get the work done on time. Push to meet your deadlines, ask for help when you need it, and don't leave a mess for someone else.
- Watch out for each other. One coworker kept a supply of snacks in her office, unlocked, as an emergency supply for a teammate that was diabetic.
- If you learn of a training opportunity that would be great for one of your office mates, share it.
- Look for ways to improve the process, the working

environment, or the product. The best innovations and cost-reduction improvements come from those who actually perform the work. Think about what you are doing, how it is currently being done, and whether there is a better way.

Recognize that showing you care is as important as actually getting the work done. Build respect and cooperation with individuals on your team and you will find that the work starts to be more enjoyable for everyone.

Chapter 7: The Foundations of Integrity and Trust

Living with integrity means: Not settling for less than what you know you deserve in your relationships. Asking for what you want and need from others. Speaking your truth, even though it might create conflict or tension. Behaving in ways that are in harmony with your personal values. Making choices based on what you believe, and not what others believe.

— Barbara De Angelis

Building Trust

Building trust in business relationships is one of the most critical factors for success. Nothing undermines a relationship more completely than lack of trust, and it cannot be taken for granted. You've heard that it takes time and effort to build trust, and only a few seconds to break it. Success in business is all about relationships, and with the proper focus you can build relationships based on trust.

Trust must be earned. When you first meet someone, they don't really know you, and so they cannot really trust you.

Don't make the mistake of assuming someone trusts you early in a relationship. Whether we admit it or not, we all tend to stereotype until we get more information about a person that either proves or disproves the stereotype. Next time you meet someone for the first time, pay attention to your thoughts about that person. You will likely be comparing him to someone else you already know and making some assumptions about this person based on those past experiences. Likewise, you do not know how you measure up because you do not know how you are being stereotyped. It is up to you to build the relationship so that your character shines and trust can be built based on who you really are.

Trust is built when people can rely on your word and it is only built through integrity and consistency in relationships. People only do business with other people that they know, like, and trust. Customers do not buy from just anybody. The popularity of the franchise restaurants is because the customer knows what kind of experience to expect, from the physical building, atmosphere and décor down to the quality and consistency of the food being served. You need to earn the trust of your customers and coworkers by letting them get to know you, your credibility, reliability, and focus on serving others.

- Do what you say you will do. Make sure you keep your promises and do not offer proposals you know you can't meet. Even the simplest items count, so if you tell your coworker you will let him know when the report is ready, make sure you do so.
- Share your expertise. Give it away, freely. Let others see that you know your subject and have the expertise to help

them as well.

- Identify the customer's needs and focus on how you can meet them. It is not about you, it is about serving them. This starts with listening to them, and making sure you understand where the gaps are that you can solve.
- Always "do the right thing." This should be the bottom line in every decision you make and action you take.

If you lead employees, you must also earn their trust and respect. Office politics, back-stabbing, negativity and lack of productivity are all symptoms of a lack of trust. Only if your team believes you have their best interests at heart will they put in the effort to achieve your business goals. Mutual trust is based on the belief that you can depend on each other to achieve a common purpose. How do you earn this trust? Here are four simple steps to get started:

1. Keep your promises.

2. Never ask someone to do something that you would not do yourself.

3. Be transparent. Share feedback, discuss priorities and goals, and communicate often.

4. Support them. Give them the resources they need, and back them up when they need you.

Trust in business relationships is critical to achieving real success. Building trust should be the focus of all your interactions, regardless of whether you are an employee, business owner or solopreneur. Become the kind of person others can count on and your reputation will grow and your success will follow.

Live With Integrity

Take the time to uncover the values that are most important to you. The first step in building your self-awareness is identifying the core values that build your own personal foundation. There are two levels to this.

Start with the overall dimensions of your life and determine which is more important to you. Here is a sample list ranked in order from a sample survey:

1. Financial
2. Family
3. Work Satisfaction
4. Personal Growth
5. Friends
6. Health
7. Home
8. Spirituality
9. Leisure
10. Leadership

You can use this list or make up your own, but the point of this exercise is to get clear on which dimensions of your life are most important to you.

The second level of values is more detailed. Here you want to really pull out the values that drive you, both personally and professionally. Do you prefer variety or precision work? Do you like making decisions? Influencing others? Stability? Are you motivated by personal achievement or affiliation with a group or a cause? You can find a list of over fifty common values to get you started on our website at http://lifechoiceexpert.com/bonuses. Your target is to whittle this down to the five values that are most important to you. A simple way to do this is to follow this three step process:

1. Read through the full list and rate each item as High, Medium or Low

2. Use the list of those items you ranked as High, and distill it down to the top ten.

3. Now, you need to drill down to the top five. The best way to do that is to start a process of comparison between each of the items. For example, let's say three of your values are recognition, health, and family. Ask yourself, would recognition be more important to you than family? Would you give up your family if it meant greater recognition? As you go through each of your comparison, you will naturally eliminate some of the choices to the point where you have identified your top five.

Congratulations! Now you have a clear list of your priorities and values to help you govern your life in a way that most suits you. Living with integrity means living your life in accordance with these values. When you don't live with integrity, it will increase your stress levels and dissatisfaction, and if left unaddressed, it will impact your health.

Ken met a popular speaker at a convention one winter. Brad, the speaker was full of energy and seemed to be on top of the world. Ken admired Brad and spent the next several months learning from him, attending his webinars, and purchasing his training courses. About six months later, Ken had an opportunity to participate in a live workshop with this speaker, and he was looking forward to absorbing more of his knowledge and energy. When the day came for the workshop to begin, Ken was shocked at the changes in Brad. Physically, he was a wreck. His posture slumped, his face was drawn with lines from long sleepless nights and his energy was gone. He'd lost so much weight that Ken's first reaction was that the speaker had been severely ill. The reality was that Brad had started a new program with his business, following the advice of others, which caused him to live out of integrity with himself. His priorities were backwards, his daily actions did not support his values, and it had taken a toll on him. His business was thriving, but Brad was not.

At work, use your priorities to help guide you in your career. Seek out work that provides you with the opportunity to live your priorities, and shy away from those that don't. Too often an employee is promoted into a job that doesn't suit him, and he accepts it because of the increase in salary and power the position offers. In this case, no one wins. The employee is in a job he dislikes, the company has lost an employee that was great at what he used to do, and there is potentially another person in the organization that would have excelled in the new position. Know yourself, know your values, and make sure you intentionally work in areas that support the person you are meant to be.

This is also a great exercise to have everyone in your work group perform and share the results. By knowing their priorities and values, you will have a frame of reference to better understand them and guide your interactions with them. For example, if you know you coworker prioritizes family over health and fitness, chances are she will be more likely to participate in a fitness event with you on Saturday if it is a family affair. At work, you can reward a coworker that values prestige and recognition by electing him to be the spokesperson for your department at the next public forum. You'll understand why your coworker who values stability is not so quick to jump on the bandwagon for the latest new proposal. It's not that he disagrees with the change; it's just that he prefers to keep the system he currently has.

Assessing Your Activities

This is likely to be one of the most painful yet most enlightening exercises you'll do. Here you are going to assess the things you do all day long to see how well you are living with integrity. The results will likely surprise you and spur you to make some changes in your life.

Pick the day you want to begin this study, and make sure you are including both workdays and non-work days. If you can dedicate yourself to doing this for a full week, you will get better results. Any individual day can be an anomaly, but a week is a good measure for how you generally tend to behave.

Start the night before, and write down your list of priorities for the next day. List those things you know you need to do, as well as those you'd really like to get done.

Each day, pull out the list from the night before, and mark down the time you've spent on each of those activities listed. Add to the list anything else you spend time on during the day, and log the amount of time spent.

At the end of the day, categorize each activity based on the 5 core values that you prioritized earlier. If that activity contributes to your value, mark it. It is fine if the same activity contributes to more than one priority. For example, leading your very first workshop for 5 of your coworkers may contribute to leadership, influencing others and variety values. If an activity does not serve any of your values, mark it as "none."

At the end of the study period, add up the amount of time for each value. Note which of your values received the most attention, and which did not. You'll also be very surprised at the amount of time you spent on activities that don't contribute to anything you hold in priority.

The goal of this study is to provide insight as to how you live your life and how much time is spent on things that are important to you. Once you've analyzed the results you'll start to see what activities should be dropped and which priorities you are neglecting. Start to make changes in your daily activities, and you will find that you are happier, more satisfied, and more engaged at work and at home.

Chapter 8: Five Things You Must Do To Be Treated Like a Professional

You are addressed by the way you dress. Your attire reflects your sense of value or taste and of course, your speech either makes or mars you.

— Jaachynma N.E. Agu, The Prince and the Pauper

Do you want to be treated like a professional? Sadly, there are employees out there that sabotage themselves from the start because they don't get the basics right. Miss these and you will not be treated the way you want to be regardless of how smart you are, how many degrees you have, or how important your work is. Hopefully this chapter is completely unnecessary for you, but perhaps there is something here you'd like to share with a teammate.

Dress and Grooming

You want to be treated like a professional? Then look like one! One good word of advice: dress according to the level you aspire to be. If you want to be promoted to manager, dress like the other managers, not the line worker in the cafeteria.

Pay attention to how others in your office dress. Even if the office allows casual dress, use some sense. Jeans may be okay, but those with bleach stains, holes, or excessive glitter are probably not. Khakis or slacks are better. Ladies, watch the jewelry and makeup. You want to be tasteful, not the center of attention. Leave the noisy bangles at home and use your daytime makeup, not what you'd wear out to a club. Pay attention to how you smell. A good rule of thumb is that no one should be able to smell you from 2-3 feet away. That means your cologne, perfume, breath, or body odor.

Tattoos and body piercings are popular, but may not be appropriate in your office. Look around you and use some sense. Be willing to cover up your tattoos and take out some of the piercings while at work. Whether you like it or not, there are some unwritten rules that you need to comply with in order to be seen as a professional.

Behavior

Keep your cool at all times. The office is not the place to shout, for any reason whatsoever. The coffee machine may have eaten your last quarter, but kicking it and shaking it is not the answer. Your coworkers don't want to live in fear of when you are going to "go off" next. Those who can keep their composure under fire are those that inspire others to listen. How many times have you seen a parent yelling at a teenager, while all the time the teenager is standing with their arms folded, rolling their eyes? It's a caricature of the person you do not want to be. When others around you are getting louder, the best way to have your voice be heard is to speak softly and slowly.

George was responsible for collecting requirements from the company's engineers across the country and working with the software developer to enhance the computer system to meet their needs. Most of the time, George was quiet, reasonable, and easy to work with. However, at random moments he would start ranting about some perceived evil that the software team had done. The lead developer had worked with George for years and was used to this. He'd learned to shrug it off and say, "That's just George." Nothing that George said in these rants was ever taken seriously or addressed, even if the concern was valid. The real damage was even more insidious. The team all knew of George's tendency to lose control and it became the subject of many jokes. George's reputation was forever tainted by his tantrums.

Save the tears. Crying makes people uncomfortable. The office is a place of business, not a place for your next therapy session. If you find yourself getting emotional, walk away. Go find a private place and get yourself under control. Your coworkers care about you, but it is not fair to them to bring your personal baggage to work. If you need help, inquire about your company's Employee Assistance Program or find yourself a therapist with the training to help you.

Watch your language. If you wouldn't say it to your mother or your preacher, don't say it at work. In today's environment, businesses are at risk for charges of harassment for your behavior. Leave out the curse words, and save the risqué stories for your buddies. You don't want to say anything that risks making your coworkers or your customers uncomfortable. Be extremely conservative here. What might seem perfectly okay to you may be offensive to someone else, particularly someone from a different generation. If you are unsure, then don't say it.

If you find yourself speaking about a situation that you don't like to someone who cannot do anything about it, you are gossiping.

Grow up. This isn't high school. There is no room for gossip or backstabbing. Your boss doesn't want to get pulled into high school drama about who was mean to you or who lied about what. If you find yourself speaking about a situation that you don't like to someone who cannot do anything about it, you are gossiping. It serves no purpose. Likewise, talking about another person behind their backs does nothing to improve the situation. This kind of behavior diminishes how others see you. If something is truly wrong and needs to be addressed, then bring it to the attention of the person who can fix it. If your coworker does something that offended you, speak directly to her. If you hear rumors about others, don't pass them along. No one wants to be the subject of the office gossip. Focus on the golden rule: treat others the way you want to be treated. Professionals address situations directly, not through office scuttlebutt. One small business owner runs her shop with no tolerance for this kind of nonsense. The moment she hears one of her employees talking behind the back of someone else, she pulls both of them into her office and makes the offender repeat what she said. Another large corporation has an even more drastic policy: you get caught gossiping you get one warning. After that, you're fired.

Punctuality

Be on time. Always. If you promise someone you will call them at 2 p.m., call at 2 p.m. Not at 2:15. Show up for meetings a few minutes early, not flying in at the last possible second and disrupting everyone. One of the most disrespectful stories is of a Director who would habitually show up for a conference call 15-20 minutes late, announce herself loudly and then ask what we are talking about. She would expect the person hosting the call to back up and explain everything that she had missed in the first 15 minutes of the call. This is just another way of disrespecting your coworkers, especially those who had made the effort to join the call on time.

There are times when you will be late and it is unavoidable. In these situations, call the person you are meeting with ahead of time and let them know. Show that you are considerate of their time and they will think highly of you for it.

Respect

Show respect for everyone. Every human being on this planet has different levels of knowledge and experiences they can bring to the table. No matter how smart you are, you can learn something from anyone. You are not superior, just different. Respect the differences and learn from them.

This is extremely important as our world becomes flatter and it is not uncommon to be working with people from different cultures. Learn about their cultures and respect them. Find out the significance behind holidays, ask about customs and style of dress, or share food from different countries. A great example of this was a manager who hosted a pot-luck dinner for her entire staff, and each person brought a dish from their home country.

No cronyism or favoritism. It is fine to be friendlier with those you like, but it is not okay to ostracize others because they don't fit into your clique. You are a team, each of you with different strengths and talents, and you must learn to work together. No boss has the patience to deal with childish antics and will not allow this to last for long in the workplace. Consider, also, that it is your responsibility to stand up for the kind of office environment you want to work in. If you see behavior that is hurtful and disruptive, take a stand against it. By ignoring it, you become part of the problem.

Preparation

Show up for work prepared. Know what your most important tasks for the day are and have your schedule planned. If you have a meeting, understand what pre-work you are expected to have done and make sure you do it. Research the subject. Bring information to share and questions to task. Be clear on what your desired outcome is from every phone call, before you pick up the phone to dial. Have all the supplies you need. Nothing shows a lack of respect and professionalism quicker than showing up unprepared.

You will find that many of your peers will just "wing it." They will come to work with no plan, read email, and then decide what to work on. They will come to a meeting without having given a moment's thought to the subject matter. By contrast, you will stand out as a superstar simply by being prepared.

Part B: Action Plan

1. Define the target.

2. What are your overall career goals?

3. What activities do you like to do, what don't you like to do?

4. Learn how to communicate more effectively.

5. Show appreciation.

6. Get to know your team on a personal level.

7. Do what you say you will do.

8. Create a success journal.

9. Evaluate yourself on the five things you must do to be treated professionally. Pick one topic each week, and focus on how well you are doing. Don't rely on your memory. Keep a log and use this to review the week and determine changes you need to make.

Part C: Taking Care of You

Chapter 9: Take Care of Yourself Because No One Else Will

The better you learn to take care of yourself, the less you settle for being around people who can't or won't treat you as well as you're accustomed.

— Curtis Sittenfeld

Does this sound like your typical day? You wake up to a blaring alarm clock, maybe hit the snooze button once or twice, and get out of bed at the last possible moment to get yourself ready and out the door on time. You stumble out of bed to start the coffee and hit the shower. After that, you rush to get dressed, maybe also rushing your kids out the door, and grab some fast food breakfast on the way. You fight your way through the traffic, or perhaps the crowds on the subway, and by the time you get to work, you're exhausted.

Lack of physical exercise, poor eating habits, no exposure to bright light, dependency on caffeine, and all that rushing and tension contribute to a decrease in metabolism, low energy and high stress.

How you wake up in the morning sets the tone for the entire day. In fact, Brian Tracy has described the morning as "the rudder of the day."

Highly successful people, those who seem to be able to do more, achieve more, and have better health, have a completely different routine. Most high achievers have tackled one of their priority items before 8am.

There are four components you should implement in your morning ritual:

1. Drink water. Your body is dehydrated when you wake up, and drinking water helps to fire up your metabolism and increase energy at a cellular level.

2. Move your body. Ever watch a cat when it first wakes up? It takes a luxurious stretch before ever even considering moving. Start your day with a long, full body stretch before you even get out of bed. Once you do get up, exercise. Some people may start their days with a full exercise session at the gym or a morning run, but if you are not used to such intensity then start with a few easy steps. Take a walk, do yoga, swim, or maybe just a few simple movements to start. The point is to get your body moving and start burning fat. You should do some form of exercise within an hour of waking up, and this will start the momentum for activity for the day. As added benefits, you burn more fat when you exercise in the morning and you will be more likely to stick with your exercise routine.

3. Eat a healthy breakfast. We all know this is the most important meal of the day, yet 30% of us skip breakfast. The rest of us usually grab something quick and usually not healthy. Take the time to fuel your body with a healthy breakfast and your energy levels will increase. It is also proven that eating a healthy breakfast is a critical component for weight loss as well. Start to experiment with quick options, such as a high-

protein, nutrient-dense shake.

4. Engage in quiet time. You should put aside quiet time by yourself to focus on your goals and your intentions for the day. What is it that you want to accomplish today? Many are believers in meditation and journaling as well. This is probably the most difficult change to make, since so many of us are not used to spending time quietly and deeply in thought. One woman spends 15 minutes outside in her yard. She says so much of her day is spent indoors that she gets energized in the morning by giving herself some time to look out at the lake, watch the sky brighten and hear the birds that are so abundant in her yard.

Consider the person who rushes through the morning and arrives at work only to take the next thirty minutes to an hour getting a cup of coffee, catching up with coworkers, checking email and figuring out what they need to do for the day. This person is reacting to the immediate activities and "busy-ness" that makes up a typical workday. The person who has taken the time to energize themselves in the morning and spent the time focusing on goals and intentions for the day will arrive at work ready to get right to the most important activities of the day. This person has figured out what the most important use of their time is and will achieve more over and over again every single day.

Even choices that seem small can make a big impact. Start by rising fifteen minutes earlier each day. Plan your breakfast to include healthier options. Stretch your body. Slowly.

Rather than make a drastic change all at once, give yourself time to build a new morning routine gradually so that you will stick with it.

Changing your morning routine will change your life. It is that powerful! Pay attention to how you start your day and begin to make small changes until you have formed these new habits.

Physical Health

You must take care of your body. You will not have the energy and stamina you need to deal with coworkers, issues, and problems at work if you have not first taken care of yourself. Your body is what carries you through the day and you must treat it right. Stress, overeating, and lack of exercise are killers. How many stories have you heard of people who allow themselves to get consumed by work, never exercise, gain a significant amount of weight over the years, and then have a major illness come crashing down on them just when they are reaching retirement age? Don't let that be you.

One very high-end executive leadership training program begins with a week-long retreat, and the very first session of the first day is focused on care of your physical body. This is so critically important that you will find most successful, high-achieving people take this very seriously.

Start by making healthier food choices. Eat a good breakfast and bring a healthy lunch to work with you rather than hitting the fast food restaurant down the road. Get educated on nutrition and adjust your diet. Keep a food log for a week and record everything you put in your mouth. At the end of the week, add up the total fat and calories you've consumed. You'll be shocked! If you need to lose weight, cut out 500 calories a day to lose a pound a week. This might be as simple as trading that high calorie, super-sized muffin at breakfast for a healthier choice. You'll find that eating lean proteins, fresh fruits, and vegetables will result in more energy and clearer thinking throughout the day.

Get moving! Take a walk, stretch, play a game of basketball, whatever it takes to give you a break from sitting at your desk all day and give your body a chance to move. Start with simple changes that you can incorporate into your day and build from there. The biggest excuse for not working out is, "I don't have time." You don't have to schedule hour long workouts at the gym. Even a ten minute walk away from your desk will help. Just don't make that walk to the cafeteria for an afternoon snack of cookies!

Make sure you get enough sleep. Your body needs rest to function at its best. If you are not getting seven to eight hours of sleep every night, make changes in your routines so that you go to bed earlier. Shut off the TV and don't bring work to bed with you. There are studies done that show that drivers that are sleep-deprived have poor reflexes and make bad decisions, and are just as dangerous as someone driving under the influence of alcohol. This holds true for work, also. Lack of sleep will impact your decision making ability, destroy your concentration, and deplete your energy levels.

Many companies understand how important it is for employees to take care of their physical health and have introduced programs to make it easier. Some even go so far as to provide the benefit of reimbursement for gym membership fees. In fact, several employees finally realized that their company really did want them to make use of the company gym during business hours when it became widely known that the President of the company used the facilities daily in the late afternoon. Lunch time workouts, on-site weight loss programs and break time games of ping pong all help you to live healthier and reduce stress. Take advantage of any such program your company has to offer, and seek out other options that suit your lifestyle.

Life Balance

In the article "Job Burnout" (Maslach, Schaufeli, & Leiter, 2001), burnout occurs when there is a disconnect between the organization and the individual with regard to six areas of work life: workload, control, reward, community, fairness, and values.

In other words, burnout is the result of being under constant pressure, working too many hours, and feeling like your job is out of your control.

Take control of your schedule and give yourself time to take breaks, exercise, spend time with family, engage in sports or spiritual activities – whatever helps you control stress and enjoy life. Motivation is easily lost if you get out of balance and don't take the time for other aspects of your life that are important to you. In today's corporate environment where teams have been "downsized" drastically, it is easy to get caught up in trying to get it all done. Likewise, business owners make the mistake of spending too much time working IN their business, not ON their business, often resulting in them having just another job where they are trading hours for dollars. Take stock of how much time you spend on different activities and compare that to what you think is really important. The more this is out of whack, the more stressed, unhappy, and unmotivated you will be.

Focus your energy on your goals.

One of the most common causes of job burnout is frustration caused by lack of progress towards an achievement. Being busy all day long without a recognizable sense of achievement demotivates and demoralizes. Put yourself into a mode of focused daily action that will lead you towards your goals. .

Get out a notepad and write down the five most important things that you need to do.

Work on those five things and don't stop until they are done. Don't go to bed, don't watch the game. Focus.

Reward yourself. Make sure you celebrate the small successes and not just wait for the day when you've finally "made it."

Remind yourself daily that activity does not equal progress. You have to have goals, and focus your energy on activities that will take you closer to those goals. Too many people are busy all the time but not on the right activities that will get them anywhere.

Establish a support system.

If you haven't read Napoleon Hill's, Think and Grow Rich, you should. Here he states that "no individual may have great power without utilizing the Master Mind", which is defined as "coordination of knowledge and effort, in a spirit of harmony, between two or more people, for the attainment of a definite purpose." In a nutshell, you need to form a team of people that you can meet with on a regular basis to support each other. You will need a support system to share your business objectives and discuss items such as:

- What are you working on?
- What did you learn?
- What do you need help with?

The support system of a Master Mind group will help with reinforcement of the good, management of the bad, and accountability for your actions. You will make a commitment to each other regarding activities you will take between meetings, and nothing does a better job of holding you accountable than the knowledge that you will need to explain the steps you took (or didn't take) in the next meeting.

Prevent overload.

We've already mentioned the importance of focusing your energies on your goals so you have a litmus test to determine what activities need to be done and which do not. You also need to learn to delegate. You cannot do everything. There is truth to the adage, 'jack of all trades, and master of none.' Use your team to spread work activities based on each other's strengths and weaknesses. What might be a struggle for you may be simple for a coworker. Understand the differences in skills that you each bring to the table and work together.

The reality is that most of us go home at the end of the day with work left undone. There just isn't enough time in the day to get it all done. You've got to make sure you focus on the most important tasks first, and ask for help if you need it.

Continuous Development

Rustout is a different kind of career death - one that is not so widely discussed. Just as your bicycle will start to rust if left outside and untended for too long, career rustout happens when you leave your career untended. When you perform the same tasks, day after day, without any thought on how to improve yourself or your contributions toward some future goal, you rust away. Your job no longer satisfies you; you lose motivation and spend your days dragging through the hours until you can leave.

Think about this....

A bar of iron costs $5
Made into horseshoes it's worth $12
Made into needles it's worth $3500
Made into balance springs for watches, it's worth $300,000
Your own value is determined also by what you are able to make of yourself.
(Author Unknown)

What are you making of yourself today?

One of the main causes of job burnout is the feeling of powerlessness you get when you just don't know how to get something done. When you feel inept, you feel a lack of control. The only way to combat this is to work on building yourself and your skills. Once you begin to feel confidence in your abilities, you are more powerful and less likely to burnout. All successful people make it a priority to work on learning new skills relevant to their chosen career paths.

Now let's talk about that commute time. Depending on whether you are driving or taking public transportation, you may currently spend this time listening to the radio, reading the paper, or perhaps chatting with fellow commuters. A better way to use this time is to listen to inspirational or educational audio programs. Load up your mp3 player with a book on tape, or a recording from a seminar, and use this time to expand your knowledge. It is said that, "the more you learn, the more you earn." The average American reads only one and a half books per year, yet they will watch thirty-five hours of television in a week! Think of the amount of knowledge you can gain by using your commute time to listen to an audio version of a book. What kind of improvements can you make in your life by expanding beyond the average one and a half books a year?

Challenge and Growth

If you're not growing, you're dying.

There is a time in a child's life, generally around 4 or 5 years old, where they learn to tie their shoes. It is a struggle at first, but with determination they can usually master it in a few short hours. Once they learn how, they will proudly show off their new-found skill over and over as they come in contact with new people over a couple of weeks. After that, the novelty wears off and they move on. You never hear them mention their shoe-tying ability again.

What if you stopped there? If you never learned to read, ride a bike, drive a car, or kiss a someone? Ridiculous, right?!

Unfortunately, there are those who perform the same job over and over every day, never learning a new skill or challenging themselves to do something different. As human beings, we all have a need to continue to improve ourselves, to feel a sense of accomplishment. At work, you can easily drift into a place where you are no longer growing. Worse, it happens gradually so that you may not notice right away that you've stagnated.

Watch out for the danger signs:

- You are the smartest person at the table. Every time.
- You can do your job with your eyes closed.
- You get no feeling of accomplishment at the end of the day.
- You haven't had to struggle in a long time to figure out how to do something.

Get into the habit of reevaluating your job at least once a year. Look for ways to incorporate a cycle of learning. This doesn't necessarily mean look for a new job. You can learn by taking on new responsibilities or encountering new situations. Cover a meeting for your boss and look for ways to expand your environment. Come up with an innovative new product or process that will impact your work team. Volunteer to put together a training course for your department. Perhaps you can start a user-focused group for customers of your products. Find ways to grow, to challenge the edges of what you thought you were capable of doing. If it makes you uncomfortable, you are stretching yourself beyond your comfort zone, and you are increasing your feelings of self-worth and self-confidence.

If you find yourself stuck in the same routine without any hope for expanding your horizons, it's time to look elsewhere. Talk to your boss about other opportunities within the company. It's in his best interest to help you. After all, you've already proven yourself to be a solid, productive employee, and you are intimately familiar with the workings of the company. Training you for a new position within the same organization benefits everybody.

There are two things you must do immediately, and revisit

on a regular basis:

1. Learn something new. Read newsletters pertaining to your industry, take a class or read a book. Find a way to increase your knowledge and your skillset.

2. Set a career goal. You've been in one place doing the same thing for too long and you've forgotten how to challenge yourself. Find something that you can strive towards that excites you. There are usually plenty of opportunities in your current job – you just need to seek them out.

Rewards

Sadly, one of the biggest failures in companies today is the failure to recognize employees for doing something right. Most of the effort is spent pointing out mistakes, attempting to "correct" weaknesses, and focusing on low performers.

We are so good at criticizing ourselves and pointing out mistakes. This is entirely backwards! Take the time to reward yourself for small accomplishments along the way and celebrate them. Did you get that presentation completed? Celebrate! Did you learn a new skill? Celebrate it! The best way to build up your confidence and your self-esteem is to document your development and your accomplishments, so that you have a running success journal. If you do this one thing consistently, you will amaze yourself at how much you accomplish by the end of the year that you would not normally have recognized.

Instead of waiting for someone else to recognize your accomplishments, celebrate your own success. When you reach a target you set for yourself, give yourself a reward. This can be as simple as building mini-rewards into your schedule. For example, schedule a coffee break right after you've finished making the 10 phone calls you are supposed to make daily. Go get a massage after you win that big contract you've been working on. Build a system of targets and rewards that you can use to measure your progress.

Toot your own horn. The larger the company, the less likely you will see recognition for the work that you do. Send an email to your boss letting him know of significant accomplishments. If your customer sends you a thank you letter, send it along to your boss. Chances are he will want to do the right thing and will forward the notifications on to his boss as well. Stand up and be noticed.

It's very important to keep a journal of your achievements in as much detail as you can. Record not only what you did, but what you had to learn, obstacles you overcame, and how you were feeling at the time. Reviewing your past achievements is one of the best methods of increasing your own self-confidence. When you are facing a new challenge, review this journal and think about the skills you had to use for projects in the past and how those skills will serve you with this new project. Anything you can do once, you can do again. Remind yourself of all the wonderful things you didn't think you could do until you actually did them. This will be a tremendous confidence booster when you stretch yourself to take on something new.

As a side benefit, you will be able to use your success journal in your performance discussions with your boss. Let's face it; most managers do a terrible job of performance reviews. It's often a task full of paperwork with company-mandated deadlines where your boss has to get everyone's reviews documented, discussed and signed off by a certain date. It's not that your boss is lazy, he's overwhelmed. Make it easy for him and provide him with the list of your accomplishments. He'll appreciate it and you'll get a better review.

All you have to do is keep a separate list of major accomplishments as they occur throughout the year, and make a note of the page number from your success journal. This will serve as your index to go back through the detailed notes without having to flip through all of the pages. You will have a concise list of accomplishments as well as a reference to the more detailed description in your journal. It takes a little bit more discipline to do this, but it will save you a tremendous amount of time when performance reviews roll around once or twice a year.

Chapter 10: How to Manage Your Inner Voice to Help You Accomplish More

Because one believes in oneself, one doesn't try to convince others. Because one is content with oneself, one doesn't need others' approval. Because one accepts oneself, the whole world accepts him or her.

— Lao Tzu

Fear

Have you ever walked on glass? Not just a single piece, but a BIG pile of glass? There was an event with a room full of people, all faced with the challenge of walking across this river of glass, and how each person dealt with this was decidedly different. They say "how you do anything is how you do everything" and so this exercise was a great example of how you deal with your fears. One woman was extremely afraid, yet she raised her hand and asked to go first. Another person moved to the end of the line and told everyone around her all the reasons why she didn't think she could do this. We saw some who gingerly took baby steps in excruciating slowness, and others who walked across briskly. With most people, the first step was the hardest. Once they took the first step to get the feel of the glass, they were able to walk through the rest of it without any fear at all.

Fear is the #1 killer of dreams.

You may be afraid that you will fail, or that you will look bad. You may be afraid to actually succeed and then have to live up to a higher expectation. If you are not feeling the butterflies in your stomach, you are not setting your dreams big enough. Everyone feels fear, no matter how successful. It is just at different levels. While one person might feel fear about speaking in front of a local networking group, another might be nervous about speaking in front of powerful business and government leaders. It's all about perspective. Don't let fear stop you. Feel the fear but do it anyway.

Procrastination

So what is the second success crusher? Procrastination!

In that same event, a woman was offered her choice of three prizes. Her husband was in the room also, and so they went back and forth trying to decide which of the three prizes she would claim. After a few minutes of this, they were given three seconds to choose, and then the next person would get to claim her choice. As you would imagine, the three seconds went by with no decision, so the second winner picked her prize. At that moment, the first winner decided that she wanted that very same prize, but it was too late. By procrastinating too long, she'd lost out on that prize. This happens all the time in life, where you analyze and think and ponder without taking action, and by the time you decide to take action the opportunity is lost.

To deal with procrastination, you need to manage yourself. What does that mean? Let's explore two different causes of procrastination and how you can manage them.

The task is too big and overwhelming.

If you know you need to do something, but it seems daunting in size or complexity, you will procrastinate. Maybe you don't have the skills, knowledge, or resources you need, so you put it off. The very best way to take this is to break the task into much smaller actions you can take to make some progress. You've heard the saying, "How do you eat an elephant? One bite at a time." For example, maybe your goal is to become a public speaker and you don't know where to start. You don't just walk out on a stage with 1,000 people in the audience. You start small, perhaps finding a local Toastmasters group in your area. Take the first step, and before you know it the rest will follow.

You don't see immediate value in it.

Here is the case where – in your mind, at least – the pain of doing the work outweighs the perceived value. Take for example, you say you want to lose weight, yet you can't pass up that piece of pie with dinner. You value the current pleasure of pie more than the future pleasure of being slim. Managing yourself means putting less focus on the immediate "want" and more on the "should" to achieve your future goals. Commit to yourself what you will achieve, and put a system in place to measure it.

To be successful in anything, you need to conquer fear and procrastination. Learn how to manage yourself even when you are feeling fearful, and take the right action anyway. Take that first step, and all the rest become easier.

Garbage In-Garbage Out

The power of words, especially those words we say to ourselves without even consciously realizing it, are the single most important factor in influencing your belief in yourself and your self-esteem. Did you know that our brains are continuously thinking at a rate of 1500 thoughts per minute, and it is estimated that 80% of those thoughts are negative?

The Second Edition of the 20-volume *Oxford English Dictionary* contains full entries for 171,476 words in current use, while the Positive Word Dictionary contains entries for 1,800 words. Is it any wonder that we are bombarded with negative messages when our language itself is only 1% positive?

Be selective about the messages you let into your brain, and seek out only those that are positive. Here are some tips on how to do this:

- Subscribe to daily motivational messages that will lift your spirits.
- Shut off the TV. Use this time instead for reading or listening to audio programs that will teach you something, or at least entertain you with positive messages.
- Surround yourself with happy people. Find others that have common goals with you, look for local groups or other successful people that will inspire you. You know that person who is always complaining, telling you how horrible her job is or how rotten her kids are? She's

sucking the energy out of you. Get her out of your life. These energy vampires are affecting your health.

Personal Qualities

In order to achieve success, there are three personal qualities you must build as a foundation. They say that success leaves clues, and if you model the behavior of successful people you can also become successful. Underneath the behavior are key characteristics of a leader that may not be evident at first glance. Master these and you are well on your way to achieving the life you want to live.

Self-Esteem

Do you believe that you are a good person? That you deserve to have good things happen to you? How about your skills? Do you think you are talented? Until you believe in yourself, you will find it very difficult to get others to believe in you.

We often have a negative talk track in our heads that continually points out our flaws in brutal honesty. Tune into your thoughts and see what I mean. You will say things like, "that's stupid," "you look fat," "why did you say that," "you'll never make that sale," etc. It's a running flow of negativity that you need to shut off. If you've ever listened to Brian Tracy, you'll recall that he coaches people to say "I like myself" over and over and over.

Self-Management

Self-management has two components: awareness and management. The first part of this is to provide yourself with an accurate assessment of your skills, strengths, and weaknesses. Remember though, you are often more critical of yourself than you should be, so take the time to get feedback from others whose opinions you trust. The second part is to set realistic goals for yourself and then keep score. Measure your progress and adjust according to that feedback. A word of caution here is to measure early and measure often so that you can make sure you are getting better every day.

Responsibility

Successful people take responsibility for themselves and everything that happens in their lives. The results you have achieved so far are directly related to the decisions and actions you've taken in life. Taking responsibility means acknowledging when you've made less than optimal choices and then doing something different. Take action towards your goals and pay attention to doing things right. Uphold your values so that you can look yourself in the mirror, and set the bar high for personal performance.

While no one can guarantee your success, the truth is that you will not be successful if you do not possess these three personal characteristics. The good news is that all of these can be learned by modeling the behaviors of others and making sure you continually give yourself honest feedback on the progress you are making.

About Mistakes

One of the concepts taught in NLP (Neuro-Linguistic Programming) is that there is no failure, only feedback. Most of us start out to do something with a presupposed outcome, and when the outcome is different we consider this to be a failure. Successful people do not consider this a failure, but rather an opportunity to learn. Thomas Edison, when asked about the thousands of failed experiments he went through to invent the carbon filament, said, "I have not failed. I've just found 10,000 ways that don't work." When you approach a mistake as an opportunity to learn something you didn't know before, you are using a positive framework. Embrace failure. Own it and learn from it and recognize that it is your choice to use this knowledge in the future.

An employee once made a mistake in a piece of software that shut down thousands of offices across the U.S. on a Saturday night and fully expected to be chewed out by his boss come Monday morning. Instead she was very calm about it, and said simply, "those who don't make mistakes are those that aren't doing anything." What an amazing outlook! Adopt this attitude for yourself, and give yourself credit for trying and stretching yourself to do something new. If the outcome isn't what you'd wanted, then take another look at the problem and see if you can see it from a different perspective with your newfound knowledge.

Chapter 11: Strategies to Get Your Workload and Your Day Under Control

Time is what we want most, but what we use worst.

- William Penn

Are you juggling too many demands on your time? Do you get to the end of your workday and feel like you haven't accomplished anything, or that you still have too much left to do?

Lack of direction, not lack of time, is the problem. We all have twenty-four hour days.

— Zig Ziglar

Imagine a bank account where every day at exactly midnight you receive $1,440. You can do anything you want with this money. The only catch is that whatever you have not spent by midnight the following day is flushed away, gone forever. It wouldn't take you long to figure out how to maximize every penny of that money, would it? You do have that "bank account", but you are not being given dollars. You are being given the gift of time. Every one of us has exactly 1,440 minutes every day, no more, no less. The super productive people you know who seem to get it all done have the same amount of time you do. The difference is how well you manage your use of those minutes.

It is said that time management is a myth. You cannot manage time, but you can manage yourself. How well are you managing your actions throughout the day to maximize the minutes spent on your highest and best activities?

Schedule Everything

Super-performers use their calendars to schedule their days. Block off the time to take care of the items that are important to you first, and then fill in the rest. Is personal fitness important to you? Schedule time on your calendar where you will go to the gym. Are you working on developing a new product that requires uninterrupted time? Schedule a conference room where you can work and put it on your calendar.

Too often, workers get in the habit of driving to work each day, checking their email, and then deciding what to work on. Take the time to do this the day before. At the end of your workday, plan out what you need to do the following day. Look at your goals, break them down into activities that you need to perform, and then schedule those activities. By making this your daily habit, you will start the day running when most people are alert and at their best, instead of trying to figure out what the most important things to accomplish that day are. If you wait until morning to do this, chances are you'll lose the best part of the day. By the time you've organized and prioritized your day, those "unplanned assignments" can creep in and you may never get to work on your priorities for the day. And of course, that leads to feelings of frustration and of being "behind."

Understand your personal energy levels and the best times for you to perform certain tasks. For instance, one executive working on a book schedules an hour every day in the early morning to write, where another businessman writes late in the evening once his children have gone to bed. Sales people know the best time of day to call their prospects, so they schedule this time every day for phone calls.

Consider location as well. Sometimes the best place for you to perform certain activities is not in your office. Maybe a conference room with a door you can close is a better place for you to make sensitive phone calls, or a picnic table outside the cafeteria will inspire you to work on that proposal you need to write. Getting out from behind your desk can often give you a fresh perspective.

Leave a block of time open to address items that you cannot plan for that just pop up during the day. You will have to guard your schedule as best you can. Life has a way of sideswiping you. You can build a perfect schedule, but business demands and emergencies can interrupt your day and throw that schedule out the window. Your boss has his own schedule, and yours will take a back seat to his demands. Your goal is to have a schedule for everything you want to accomplish, and use this as your guiding principle for the day. If an emergency arises that can't be ignored, readjust your schedule. Overall the habit of planning and scheduling your day will continue to move you closer to your goals, even if you get sideswiped once in a while.

Let it Ring

Just because the phone rings doesn't mean you have to answer it. Consider this philosophy: the phone rings at a time that might be convenient for the caller but not necessarily for you. Now that we have caller ID and customizable ring tones, you can easily filter out the short list of people that you want to react to immediately (your kid's school, an aging parent…). The rest can leave a message that you can respond to when it is convenient for you. If you are using a schedule to maximize your day, you don't want to throw it out the window every time the phone rings. Another option for those who can afford it is to have a "gatekeeper" to answer and filter phone calls for you.

Are you one of those people that call back phone numbers that register on your cell phone but don't leave a message? Why do you do that? If the caller didn't leave a message, then it isn't important enough to waste your time on. If you dial a wrong number and realize it just as the phone starts to ring, do you really want that person to call you back to find out who you are and why you were calling? Is that a good use of your time?

Take the Email Challenge
For an entire day, keep count of the number of
times you hit "send/receive" in your email.
If you have your email sync'd automatically
to your phone or other device, count how
many times you look at your inbox. You'll
be shocked!

Put Email in Its Place

Email is a convenience we've grown accustomed to, but one of the biggest time wasters as well. If you keep your email windows open, your attention will drift there whenever you are stuck with something, procrastinating about a task you don't want to do, or just feel compelled to see who sent you something. Having an open email window is like having a bright shiny box sitting in front of you with a note that says "do not look at me!" You just can't keep yourself from looking. Close it down, mark some time in your schedule for email, and then and only then you can go read through all your emails.

As for keeping the email under control, lots of information has been written on this subject but the best thing you can do is establish a rule to only touch it once. Each email should be trashed, filed away for information purposes that you might need later, or acted upon. If you can't act upon it right away, find a tickler system that works for you. Perhaps you create a folder just for items you need to do, add it to your task list, or use a system to flag these. Don't just leave it to linger in your inbox. Do everything as quickly and as effectively as you can and be ruthless about trashing those emails that really aren't important.

To Do Lists

As silly as it sounds, there is something satisfying in crossing items off a list. It is a concrete, tangible action that makes you feel good about yourself, like you've accomplished something.

Keeping a list helps you focus, but a better system is to

keep two lists:

Create a master list of everything you can think of that you think you need to do. Everything. Your kid wants to go shopping for new shoes? Add it to the list. You promised someone you met at a networking meeting that you'd share a contact? Add it to the list. The point of this exercise is to get everything out of your head. The more you are keeping these items in your head, trying to remember everything, the more you are unable to focus on the things that are really important. Keep one and only one *master* list. If you keep one list on your smart phone, another in your notebook next to your bed, and a third in your CRM software, you'll drive yourself crazy. Find a tool that works for you and keep it with you.

This list will end up being very large, but you may never actually do some of the items you put on here. The point of this exercise is to allow you to see the whole picture, everything that you were juggling in your head, and pick out those things that are truly important. You'll find over time that some items just fade in significance or get completed by someone else so that you never really needed to address them anyway.

Spend a few minutes at the end of your day writing a list of the most important tasks that you need to do *tomorrow*. Some people prefer to do this in the morning, but the it is much better to do this the night before. This helps you get your day started with the right mindset and keeps you focused. Rather than starting your day working on creating the list of things to do, you can jump right in and get started. One word of caution: Keep this list small. Only write down a handful of important things and don't make a laundry list of every possible thing you can think of that you need to do. That's the point of the master list, not this one. You do not want to be carrying items from one day to the next. You want the satisfaction of crossing off those 4 or 5 items at the end of the day and saying, "I'm done!"

While you are spending time planning your activities for tomorrow, also use this time at the end of the day crossing items off your master list that you'd completed that day. This helps you keep your master list up-to-date with items you've completed. The natural inclination is to cross items off the master list as soon as you add them to your daily list, but this would be a mistake. We all have days when we don't accomplish everything we set out to do, so you want to keep this as an active item on your master list until you know for sure that it is done.

Eliminate Interruptions

Sounds wonderful, doesn't it?

Maria says: I work from home and I still haven't figured out how to keep my kids out of my office after school is over, or how to stop my husband from asking me questions all day long. I tried setting rules but no one thinks the rule applies to them. Their situation is somehow special. I've tried gesturing to be quiet when I am on the phone, but that just makes them whisper at me instead of speaking in a normal voice. I've tried shutting the door, getting angry, threatening to go back to a "real office," and none of it works. Here is where I need your help so please let me know if you have any suggestions for me!

The reality is that you cannot control anyone else's behavior but your own. How do you react to someone interrupting you? Do put aside what you are working on to focus on them? If so, you are encouraging the interruption. Control your schedule and defend it. Obviously there are situations that are urgent enough where you want to be interrupted, but generally you need to train those around you to respect your time. If you work from home, block off 15 minutes when your children get home from school to connect with them. When your coworker comes by to talk to you, let him know you are busy with something and you are available at 4:30. Turn your back to the room when you are on the phone. Shut your door as a signal to others that you are not to be disturbed, but make sure you open it back up again when it is okay for them to approach you. You don't want to be behind closed doors 100% of the time. Carve out time you need for uninterrupted work and make it known to those around you. As long as you balance that with time when you are available, you will find over time that others will learn to respect your wishes.

It's unrealistic to expect that you will never be interrupted, but by taking deliberate actions you will find that interruptions can be minimized.

Multitasking

Somewhere along the way, we started to believe that the ability to multitask, to work on more than one thing at the same time, was both admirable and desirable. Women, especially, pride themselves on how much they can juggle at once.

Wrong.

Multitasking is just another form of interruption. Only this time, it is you that is interrupting yourself.

Let's put the simple tasks aside. We're not talking about the ability to walk and chew gum at the same time. We can handle adding a task that can be done unconsciously without interrupting the things you actually have to think about. It's okay to listen to music while cleaning off your desk. The type of multitasking we are concerned with is when you have more than one project to work on simultaneously that requires you to focus.

The human brain does not have the ability to work on more than one thing at a time. Instead, it switches back and forth between tasks in a process called context-switching. The more complex the tasks, the more time is lost in context switching.

Here's a simple example:

You're writing a proposal outlining the pros and cons of alternate approaches, and your boss asks you for last month's expense report. You turn your attention to your boss's request and start searching for the report. Luckily it is already done, so you just have to find it and send it over. Now you can turn your attention back to the proposal you were working on. Unfortunately, now you've lost your train of thought. Now you need to review what you'd already written and figure out which points you'd covered and where to pick up the thread. The amount of time it takes you to get back to where you were before you turned your focus to the expense report is completely lost, unproductive time. You would have been able to complete both tasks quicker if you'd finished the proposal before searching for your expense report.

To illustrate, Task A and Task B will each take 15 minutes

to complete if done serially. You spend 2 minutes putting all the materials from Task A away, and gathering your thoughts and the materials you need for Task B. This is time lost for switching context.

Total time elapsed in this scenario is 32 minutes:

The human brain doesn't multi-task like a computer. It doesn't switch from one task to the next effortlessly. Instead, it thrashes back and forth with time lost in between to get our thoughts together about where we left off and understand the context of what we need to accomplish. The constant effort this requires means that doing even just two or three things at once puts far more demand on our brains compared with if we did them one after another. If we work on those same two tasks from our previous example, but attempt to work on them at the same time, the time elapsed might look more like this:

For purposes of this example, let's assume it takes 2 minutes each time you switch between Task A and Task B for you to get your thoughts together about what you need to do, where you left off, and where the materials are that you need. In this case, you'll be switching between Task A and Task B 13

times, so you will waste 26 minutes overall just getting into gear to start the work each time you switch. That's almost twice as long as it would have taken if you had just completed one task before working on the second.

When we try to concentrate on two tasks at once, we essentially put our brains on overload. Have you ever felt stressed and anxious to get too many things done at once? It leads to a vicious cycle where we feel overloaded yet compelled to multi-task even more because there is so much we have to do. You lose even more time to context switching, increase your levels of anxiety, and as a result, accomplish less.

An American study reported in the *Journal Of Experimental Psychology* found that it took students far longer to solve complicated math problems when they had to switch to other tasks - in fact, they were up to 40 per cent slower.

The best approach, then, is to stop multi-tasking and focus on one thing at a time. Pick up a task and work at it until you either complete it or reach a natural stopping point where you need to wait for something or someone else. If you need to put that task aside and pick it up later, make a notation to yourself about where you left off. This will help you get back to the same place when you come back to this task later.

Meetings

Ah... meetings.

No one really likes attending meetings, but they seem to multiply. Like nature abhors a vacuum, new meetings seem to pop up just when you think you finally have some free time on your calendar to get some work done. The changing dynamics of the workplace and amazing innovations in technology have made the office where all your coworkers are in the same physical location at the same time a thing of the past.

Organizations have flattened out, so your boss may be halfway across the continent rather than down the hall. Companies hire subcontractors that work in their own office locations, teammates work from home, and globalization has us working with others in countries around the world. While this dynamic is exciting, getting decisions made in a casual conversation in the hallway or bringing the team into a conference room to brainstorm on a whiteboard are no longer possible. All of this has led to a proliferation of meetings as a means of communicating, sometimes appropriately but most of the time, not so much.

How many of you have walked out a meeting saying "what a waste of time"? Or had to suffer through a second meeting where all that was discussed was a rehash what was discussed at the previous meeting?

An upcoming technician found herself in the position where she had some specialized domain knowledge that was critical to the success of a major corporate objective. For the first time in her career, she was invited to participate in a two day conference with all the major stakeholders for this project. Executives from different parts of the company were flying in to attend this meeting to lay out the strategy. She was excited! She had never participated in anything like this, and couldn't wait to be part of this groundbreaking discussion. The day finally arrived, and she sat in the conference room with Directors, Executive Directors, even a VP or two, hour after hour discussing the project. At the end of the day, she went home to her husband and noted that not much had been accomplished, and it didn't seem like they'd focused on any one particular area, but maybe this first day was supposed to be that way. Maybe the point was to get everyone to the same level of understanding. Surely, tomorrow would be the big day where the roadmap got laid out for the future.

The second day, she again sat in the meeting, hour after hour, becoming more puzzled as the day wore on. Finally, as the other participants started looking at their watches to calculate what time they had to leave for the airport to make their flights home, the conversation came to a halt. One of the executives looked around the room and asked, "So what did we decide?" Silence. Sheepishly they realized that they had danced around the problem for two days and had not decided anything. They had to admit that they needed to get back together again to tackle the problem. The technician was astounded! When her husband asked what had been decided, she replied, "All they decided was to decide later!"

Not all meetings run amok as blatantly as that one had, but companies everywhere have problems with unproductive meetings.

Your solution is to become a meeting expert!

Start with a rough calculation of cost. The next time you think you need a meeting, estimate the average hourly salary of the people that need to participate to arrive at the cost of that meeting just in terms of labor costs. Don't forget to factor in travel costs (airfare, mileage) if the meeting is on-site rather than virtual. Of course, that doesn't take into account lost productivity or opportunity cost, as well as any potential expenses for the meeting facility, food, etc. Now that you have a number, think about the purpose of the meeting. Does it warrant the cost? In other words, if the meeting accomplishes what you set out to do, will the meeting have a positive return on investment (ROI)?

You've got to control all aspects of the meeting. A meeting amateur jumps right in and schedules a meeting as soon as she hears a meeting is needed. There are actually four phases to every meeting, and the meeting expert controls each of them.

Phase 1: Planning

Have a clear purpose for the meeting. If there is no clear purpose, cancel it. Meetings have a way of breeding other meetings, and if you are not careful you may find yourself with a calendar full of recurring meetings that don't seem to accomplish much. One team kept a standing weekly meeting on the calendar to meet with the legal team, since they were so hard to schedule on an ad hoc basis. They managed this by polling the project leads each Friday to solicit agenda items for the next meeting. By Monday morning, the owner of the meeting would either have a list of items to address or the meeting that week was cancelled.

Document the agenda. Review with those you need input from and make sure the agenda contains all the items needed to achieve the stated purpose. The number one cause of meeting failure is a lack of a clear agenda.

Decide in advance who needs to participate. Is this an information sharing session where the whole team needs to be invited? Or is there a problem that needs to be addressed that requires certain key personnel to help find the solution?

Schedule in advance so that key participants are available to attend. Poll them if you must and make sure the people you need are available during your proposed date and time. Solicit multiple options and consolidate the responses to find the best time for all.

Phase 2: Preparation

Reserve facility, conference-call line or other resources as needed. You don't want any last-minute scrambling that cuts into the time you have scheduled for the discussion. One of the most common mistakes is neglecting to make sure the conference bridge has enough ports for the expected number of participants.

Send invitations with the agenda as well as clear expectations of any pre-work required. Eliminate the dreaded "dead air" when you ask for input. You want people to show up ready to discuss the items on the agenda, not spend the time "getting up to speed." Unfortunately, too often people are busy juggling multiple priorities so the only time they focus on your particular project is when they are in a meeting with you. Let them know what is expected of them in advance.

Phase 3: Execution

Start and end on time. No exceptions. Respect the time of those who are participating and start when you say you will start. Start and end on time. No exceptions. Respect the time of those who are participating and start when you say you will start. Remember, if there are those who show up late, don't spend time getting them up to speed on what you've already covered. That's disrespectful to the team members who were there on time. Of course if that tardy team member is a C-level position, you may need to rethink this position.

Give yourself permission to end a meeting early. Too often meetings drag on to the set amount of time allocated, whether the team has anything useful to discuss or not. Once you've accomplished the meeting purpose, end it. Your team will appreciate the gift of recovered time. One project manager had a monthly meeting with the CIO where she provided an update on a particular program. This was a regularly scheduled meeting allocated for 45 minutes every month. Eventually the program stabilized and it happened that there was a month where there wasn't much new to report. The project manager provided a short update, and was done in 20 minutes. Rather than dragging out the conversation to cover the allotted 45 minutes, and wasting everyone's time, she ended the call and the CIO was glad to have the time back.

Control the conversation. Make sure the team stays on track and no side items are discussed. Focus on the agenda. If someone interjects with a new agenda item, let them know that you will be happy to work with him to arrange another meeting to address it. Chances are you don't have all the right players in the meeting to discuss that item anyway.

Close the conversation with a recap of the decisions made and next steps. This allows you to get final confirmation from everyone in the meeting on what was agreed to.

Phase 4: Follow-up

Document the meeting. Include the names of the participants, major discussion points, decisions reached, and action items that need to be addressed after the meeting.

Share the meeting minutes with all stakeholders, not just those that attended the meeting. This will reduce the number of "bystanders" in your meeting (see below).

Follow-up on all action items until they are resolved.

Here are some common problems you may experience and suggestions on how to handle them.

A critical resource does not join the meeting.

Of course, you had already cleared with him that he was available at this time, he accepted your meeting invitation, yet he does not show up. Perhaps he forgot or just got sidetracked with something else he is working on.

Your first step is to attempt to contact him. Call his cell phone, send him a text message, or ask someone who works with him if they've seen him. Contact his boss to see if he is in the office that day or called away on an emergency.

If that is unsuccessful, poll the people in your meeting if there is anything you can accomplish towards the goal without the missing person. Perhaps he is needed for part of the conversation but there are other parts that can continue without him.

If the meeting can't continue, end it. Apologize and let them know you will reschedule.

Afterwards, establish personal contact with the key resource. Make sure he is aware that the conversation had to be tabled in his absence, and get him to commit to a new date/time.

The conversation takes longer than expected.

You've scheduled the meeting for an hour, kept the team focused on the agenda, but they just need more time to finish the discussion. You have two choices:

End the meeting on time and set up a follow-up meeting. Consider that by scheduling a meeting for a set amount of time, you have permission to use that time on their calendars. You have no idea what they may have scheduled after your meeting.

Poll the team and ask how much longer they need to finish the discussion and whether they are available to continue on past the scheduled ending time. This option should only be used when all the participants are in agreement. Too often the most vocal players vote to stay and the quieter ones are forced to adjust something else on their schedule. Make sure this is a unanimous vote.

The number of participants in your meeting expands well beyond what you expected, or need.

As the number of participants increases, so does the cost of your meeting. Will allowing uninvited people to attend keep the ROI of your meeting in the black?

As people join your meeting, ask them to introduce themselves and their role. If someone announces they are just there to "listen in," let them know that you will be sending out meeting minutes and their participation is not required. Be polite but firm. This generally occurs when someone is interested in the subject matter and wants to learn more, or they feel that they will be uninformed if they do not attend the meeting.

A VP had a standing meeting every Tuesday with his direct reports and the Program Management Office (PMO), where he reviewed the entire portfolio of active projects and any hot topics that were hindering progress. These conversations became so detailed that the Executive Directors started to invite their Directors to attend, who started to invite the Managers, who then started to invite the Technical Leads for each of the active programs. Before they knew it, the attendance at this meeting had grown to 60-70 people every week. What would it do to your budget to have a meeting with almost ten times the number of participants than you required? Most of the time, only the same seven or eight people did the talking, but no one ever could predict what detailed knowledge was going to be required to address the next question. Also, what they found was that the expanded list of attendees wanted to be there because this was the only forum where they had exposure to the VP to hear what his priorities were, and only the only forum where they were able to hear what else was happening in the department.

Use technology. With today's conference calling features, you can see phone numbers of who has dialed into your call. As they announce, associate names to phone numbers. A good practice to get into is to read the list of attendees after everyone has announced and ask if you missed anyone. If they don't announce, let them know one final time that you will be removing them from the bridge if they don't announce, and then do it. They'll get the message.

Participants don't seem to be getting it.

Remember, communication is not what was said, it is what was received. Make sure the participants are truly communicating.

Too often conversations go on where two people are "talking past each other." This happens when they are not clear on what the other is saying, so they've made a false assumption. Interject with an explanation to help bring clarity to both parties.

Watch for "violent agreement." This happens when you've got two parties energetically defending their positions thinking they are in opposition when in fact they are both arguing for the same thing, just stated differently.

If you see resistance to an idea, make sure it is not due to confusion. Keep in mind that some people may be able to hear a new idea and understand it, while others need some sort of visual cues to help them assimilate new information. A financial analyst, generally open to process improvements in her department, continued to resist an idea that would carve days out of the time it took her team to perform a task. No one could understand why she was objecting to something that was clearly so beneficial to her department. Finally, they drew a process diagram showing the current process, and then the new and improved process. The moment she saw the diagrams, she understood the proposal and agreed immediately. There is truth to the old adage, "the confused mind says no."

Address cultural differences.

There are societies where employees will agree with the boss, no matter what. They may not understand what is being said, or agree with it, but they will say "yes" regardless. Of course, once the meeting is over you'll find that whatever was agreed to doesn't get done.

Put a Price Tag on It

Not literally of course. But time really is money, and you should calculate the value of your time. If you are employed and receive a paycheck, then you already know how much your employer values an hour of your time. Simply divide your annual salary by 2080 (40 hours a week x 52 weeks = 2080) and that will give you an hourly rate for a full time job. If you are self-employed, here's a formula to use:

Step 1:

Establish the target income you would like to make this year. For example, let's say you want to earn $100,000.

Divide that target by 2080 hours (the number of hours worked in a year). For our example, $100,000 / 2080 = $48.08.

This is the amount of money you need to earn each hour to meet your goal. Are you working on activities every hour of every week all year long that bring you in revenue? Probably not. Instead, let's recalculate a more realistic answer by only accounting for hours you are working on revenue-generating activities.

Step 2:

Use the same target income you established above. Again, we'll use $100,000.

Calculate the number of hours you are actually working on activities that bring in revenue. That means you cannot count hours spent goofing off, surfing the internet, or performing administrative duties. A good rule of thumb is that you will spend about three hours a day on revenue-generating activities. The calculation looks like this:

50 weeks a year x 5 days a week x 3 hours a day = 750 productive hours

Divide your target revenue by the number of productive hours to get your true hourly rate. In our example, $100,000 / 750 = $133.33

This is the true value of an hour of your time if you are to meet your income goals.

Now, before you take on anything new, ask yourself these questions:

- Is the time spent on this activity going to make you enough money to meet your income target?
- Will this help you learn something useful that will increase your ability to earn money in the future or improve your career options?
- Is this something that will help you achieve a long-term goal?
- Is this something you want to do because it's fun and you are okay with allocating time to it? Remember, life is about balance so make a conscientious effort to put in your life the things you consider to be fun.
- Does this need to be done to cover the basic care and feeding of your family? Things like grocery shopping and taking a kid to the dentist fall into this category.

If you can't answer yes to at least one of those questions, find a way to get out of it. Learn to say no and mean it.

We all have to battle the constant demands on our time and everyone finds their own techniques for doing this.

Part C: Action Plan

1. Establish a calm morning routine.

2. Take care of your health.

3. Learn something new. Read newsletters pertaining to your industry, take a class or read a book. Find a way to increase your knowledge and your skillset.

4. Create a success journal.

5. Pay attention to your self-talk.

6. Clean up your email habits.

7. Focus on one task at a time.

8. Get meetings under control.

To laugh often and much; to win the respect of intelligent people and the affection of children; to earn the appreciation of honest critics and to endure the betrayal of false friends. To appreciate beauty; to find the best in others; to leave the world a bit better whether by a healthy child, a garden patch, or a redeemed social condition; to know that even one life has breathed easier because you have lived. This is to have succeeded.

— Ralph Waldo Emerson

CAREER C.H.O.I.C.E. SYSTEM

I would like to say thank you for purchasing this book by offering you an exclusive deal.

Are you where you want to be in life? Are you happy with your career choice? Do you have the financial security you always wished for? Or perhaps you feel like there is more out there for you, that you are not living up to your full potential, and you are just not sure how to get it.

There is no better time than now to improve and transform your life. Never before have we been so stressed out, burned out and worked so hard only to feel it taking a toll on our health, relationships and the quality of our lives.

You have a C.H.O.I.C.E! Join me and learn the Career C.H.O.I.C.E. system to get your life back.

With this value-packed program, you will walk away with your very own custom definition of success in your terms that you can put into practice immediately.

- Take control of your career and your future
- Learn powerful techniques for tackling the overwhelmed "to do" list
- Find out how to tell what you really want and how to stop sabotaging yourself
- Breathe new life into your old dreams and desires
- Build confidence in yourself and your abilities
- Chart your own action plan to greater balance, happiness,

achievement and joy in life

Learn who you were meant to be, what you need to do to get there, and finally have the life you really deserve!

So what's the deal?

This is a 7 part program. Because you have purchased my book, I am inviting you to attend the first session free.

AND...

If you like what you hear and want to participate in the rest of the program, you will be able to do so at a **substantially reduced price**. All you have to do is listen to the first session all the way to the end to find out how you can take advantage of this offer.

Let's talk about where you are and where you want to be so we can brainstorm ideas to get you there. To register, go to http://lifechoiceexpert.com/special-bonus/

ABOUT THE AUTHOR

 Joanne is a speaker, author, and consultant and is a widely recognized expert in aligning teams to perform with purpose. She brings the knowledge and skills that help business owners implement simple but time-tested strategies to get results faster and more efficiently. Joanne has honed her skills in Fortune 500 companies such as Verizon and IBM, where she led large projects with team members from all around the world, steering them through the process from project initiation through completion. In addition, Joanne has consulted with small business to design business and people structures for organizational effectiveness.

Joanne has extensive experience in leading global, virtual teams and has demonstrated leadership with diverse work teams. She has more than 25 years of experience in the corporate environment with strong focus on IT and Telecommunications.

She is currently CEO and Founder of Nashville Success Summit, a premier membership community for small business owners.

Joanne lives with her husband, Paris in Nashville, Tennessee. Both her son, Anthony, and her daughter, Alexis, are students at Florida State University.

Connect With Joanne

Web	http://LifeChoiceExpert.com/
	http://www.linkedin.com/in/joanneeckton
	https://www.facebook.com/lifechoiceexpert
	http://twitter.com/#!/JoanneEckton